*P*ARKER *T*YLER

the three faces

New and Revised Edition

SOUTH BRUNSWICK
NEW YORK: A. S. BARNES AND CO.

the three faces of the film

Parker Tyler was born in New Orleans in 1907. During most of his adult life he has been a foremost influence as a critic in the field of fine arts. He was an editor of *View* Magazine from 1942 to 1947, and for the following three years wrote film chronicles for *The Kenyon Review*. From 1954 to 1959 he was Editorial Associate and contributor to *Art News,* and Managing Editor for two of its Annuals. His writings have appeared in many literary and art magazines. A poet as well, in 1958 he received a Longview Award for poetry. But Mr. Tyler's most important work has been in the field of film criticism, and since the appearance of his first book, *The Hollywood Hallucination*, in 1944, probably no other film critic in the world has received so many accolades or been quoted so often. He has also, for many years, lectured and been a program commentator for the New York film society, Cinema 16. Among Mr. Tyler's other books are *Magic and Myth of the Movies, Chaplin,* and *Yesterday's Children*.

of the film

THE
ART

THE
DREAM

THE
CULT

LONDON: THOMAS YOSELOFF LTD

A. S. Barnes and Co., Inc.
Cranbury, New Jersey

Thomas Yoseloff, Ltd
18 Charing Cross Road
London W. C. 2, England

6591
Printed in the United States of America

acknowledgments

For permission to reprint all but three of the following articles, which are hitherto unpublished, thanks are due these magazines and publishers:

The American Quarterly, for "Hollywood as a Universal Church," copyright 1950 by *The American Quarterly*.

Portfolio, for "The Atomic Age at New York's First Film Festival," copyright 1964 by *Art News* division of Newsweek, Inc.

Art News, for "The Artist Portrayed and Betrayed," copyright 1954 by *Art News*.

Arts Digest, for "The Film Sense and the Painting Sense," copyright 1954 by Parker Tyler.

Cinema 16, for "*Rashomon* as Modern Art," copyright 1952 by Cinema 16.

Film Culture, for "The Lady Called A," and "For Shadows, Against Pull My Daisy," copyright 1962 and 1963 by *Film Culture*.

Forum, for "Movies and the Human Image," copyright 1958 by *Forum*.

The Kenyon Review, for "Film Form and Ritual as Reality," copyright 1948 by *The Kenyon Review;* "Reality into Dream into Myth into Charade into Dollars," copyright 1951 by *The Kenyon Review;* and "On the Cult of Displaced Laughter," copyright 1958 by *The Kenyon Review*.

Partisan Review, for "The Movies as a Fine Art," copyright 1958 by *Partisan Review*.

The Sewanee Review, for "The Dream-Amerika of Kafka and Chaplin," copyright 1950 by *The Sewanee Review*.

The author is in special debt to various avant-garde film makers who took the trouble to supply exactly the stills required to illustrate their work here, he also wishes to extend cordial thanks to Mr. Gideon Bachmann for making available a number of items from his extensive library of stills, and to all those institutions and individuals who gave permission to reproduce art works from their collections as well as to all the film distributors who cooperated in the same way. For special courtesies, additional thanks are due Mr. Amos Vogel, director of the New York Film Festival, and to Cinema 16.

contents

illustrations

THE ART

THE DREAM

9

Prehistoric Hand
Alphaville
Last Year at Marienbad
Shadows
The Mirage

THE CULT

The following illustrations appear as a group after page 112
Crossfire
Les Liaisons Dangereuses
Sweet and Sour
Shadows
Rodin: *Orpheus and Eurydice*
de Chirico: *Troubadour*
Brancusi: *Socrates*
Miro: *Group of Women*
Duchamp: *La Mariée mis à nu par ses célibataires, même*
Léger: *Le Grand Déjeuner*
Tchelitchew: *Hide and Seek*
Marca-Relli: *The Strategist*
Ivan the Terrible
The Dybbuk
Narcissus
The Red and the Black

The "Hollywood Hallucination" Rampant: an Introduction

In his trenchant book, *Individualism Reconsidered*, David Riesman ended one of his chapters by casually evoking what he termed "the Hollywood Hallucination"; the phrase, as he knew, was the title of a book I had published in 1944. It would have been difficult to say that the term, because of Riesman's ephemeral adoption of it, had entered the language, or even the vocabulary of film criticism. Since the year of my book's publication, I had tried to advance from the position I took in it: that the popular ritual of movie-going had a number of tangible rewards having little to do with a given film's intended merits. Not the least of such auxiliary, gratuitous merits was the spectator-experience I compassed by the term "hollywood hallucination." Turning it into lower-case is not my idea, but that of a very recent writer in *The Village Voice* (New York) who even uses it in the plural. So the H. H., evidently, has survived in the vocabulary of film criticism.

I took no trouble in 1944 to define the limits of the experience contingent on this term. On the contrary, I had accepted all movie-going as primarily a Surrealist binge whose object was to appreciate all the points about the human imagination which got into films, so to speak, through the back doors of the studios. Such points were assumed to form part of the conscious and sub-conscious life of all human fantasy, whether in dreams or in the movies. The only *indubitable* reading of a given movie, therefore, was its value as a charade, a fluid guessing game where all meanings made an open quantity, where the only "winning answer" was not *the* right one but *any* amusingly relevant and suggestive one: an answer which led to interesting speculations about society, about mankind's perennial, profuse and typically serio-comic ability to deceive itself. In short, the commercial movie was a automatist self-portrait of the common man, and perhaps of his betters too.

Naturally, as sub- and semi-conscious, all this "dream material" in the films lacked what might be called clear definition and verifiable limits. Later on, Professor Suzanne K. Langer essayed to define the *dreamlike* nature of film as an expressive medium. And two writers produced books titled *Holly-*

wood: the Dream Factory (Powdermaker) and *The Dreamers and the Dream* (Alpert). But most of both books, like Professor Langer's academic definition, fall outside the lines I laid down, while thematically and conceptually, of course, they bear a general relation to my main premises. I was by no means the first to suggest the folk-myth quality of popular films or that the movies betokened a mass "metaphysic." I simply investigated and formulated, drawing on psychoanalysis and my own ingenuity. Psychoanalysis was involved partly because even commercial movies were growing, during the forties, psychology-conscious. Even so, I preferred showing the nature of the spectator's practice rather than the actual terms of the film-makers' premises. The grand anticlimax of the latter has been Federico Fellini's two biographic fantasies (*8½* and *Juliet of the Spirits*) which consciously blend pure spontaneous fantasy with the trick resources and native visual splendor of the filmic medium. The spectator's sophisticated pastime has turned into the big film-maker's deliberate premise. Fellini the director is himself an "irresponsible" dreamer—or so, deviously, he makes it *seem*.

Eric Bentley's public remarks about my books sanctioned that original viewpoint of mine as significant and fertile. I never thought of carrying the argument into journalism or doing more than "making it" with the literary quarterlies. Most of my later activity with this type of film criticism was in the latter forties, when another volume, *Magic and Myth of the Movies*, appeared. Not surprisingly, there was a contingent (even in the literary quarterlies) that considered my exploitation of my themes, after a certain saturation point, frivolous and unfair to the "art" of the movies; unfair partly because, in making Hollywood a symbol of botched art, I was being somewhat unpatriotic. Undoubtedly I have not been, by a long shot, the world's most *constructive* film critic. In the present book, which first appeared in 1960, I tried to systematize my attitudes by concentrating on three main approaches to the world of film-making, approaches based on fields where the movies seem to have staked out, sometimes indiscriminately, their own peculiar ground: in art, in cult, in dream.

But, by 1960, my early books had seemingly been sown in a field where a strange aftermath was currently blossoming. The canon promulgated as elite movie-going in the forties was becoming, two decades later, a brand of elite movie-making. The slant on which I had first concentrated was now taking hold with people who *made* films rather than with people who *looked at* them. The fact that—via clique, cult, and lots of loose daydreaming—this was happening even in the large studios, meant that ground previously held sacred to the serious avant-garde and experimental films was being trespassed upon. Thus a revised edition of the present book seemed called for. Now, when the Nouvelle Vague of Truffaut, Resnais, and Godard continues to look chic, and correspondingly the old avant-garde of Cocteau, Buñuel, and Dali logically looks old-hat, it is time to underline the whys and wherefores.

12   Historically, beginning with Cocteau's *The Blood of a Poet*, there had been a sparse tendency to identify film fantasy with the art operation itself, the *hero* being (unlike the lunatic Caligari) an *artist*. When Fellini, however, did his *8½*, it was imperfectly recognized that this film was a popularized expansion of the situation in Cocteau's 1930 film: an artist's inner ordeal. Meanwhile, Hans Richter, a radically and culturally minded German film maker, had made in the forties a Surrealist-mannered film, *Dreams That Money Can Buy,* which offered situation-variations on the styles of several modern painters: Léger, Max Ernst, Duchamp. The commercial film, though it proceeded to do biographies of important artists (Gauguin, van Gogh, Toulouse-Lautrec, and Michelangelo), took the pedestrian attitude of ordinary biography, dressed up in fiction stereotypes but duly showing the artist's ordeal: one of the chapters in the present book deals with the vulgarities and slanders of this commercial genre.

Inevitably, films meant for wide popular distribution (however eminent the film-maker) steer away from straight fantasy of the Surrealist type and keep to a semblance of "reality." On the other hand, daydreaming fantasy, with its roots in subconscious desire, has always had an insistent life among spectators, whether or not formulated as I had formulated it. One knew very well that the phantasmal improbability of horror melodramas was the commercial product catering to and dominating the common impulses of popular taste; such factors, of course, supply only the rudiments of the Surrealist *game* of sophisticated movie-going. But the European continent is better at organizing its élite culture, in whatever field, than is the United States or England. In the last fifteen years, new literate and quasi-adult standards have been established for the film of fantasy and for an extra dimension of reality in dreamlike or trancelike experiences.

Last Year at Marienbad marked an impressive step in this direction. Yet this film by the novelist Alain Robbe-Grillet and the director Alain Resnais has a French elegance and nuance that delimit its mass appeal. Even in France, a tendency existed to regard it as a daring and sophisticated stunt— which, (alas!) is about all it is. An important thing about it was that, like Fellini's biographic-fantasy films, it bore strong birthmarks of avant-garde technique and an obvious concession to the existence of a visionary world where reality is neither common sense nor representational. It sounds a bit barbarous to say so (and somewhat like Japanese English) but *Last Year at Marienbad* was one very chic *hollywood hallucination.*

To an impressive degree, the film was given over to "effects" that, while technical and artificial from the usual standpoint, draw substantially from the established idiom of the small experimental films of the European and American avant-garde. An outstanding figure of this group is the late Maya Deren, whose brief films are pure cinema in that they are based squarely upon the "magical" function of ordinary film devices: slow motion, stop-camera, reversed and telescoped time, extreme angles, multiple exposure. These, however, are not incidental effects in her films but rather shape trance action and

13

the private fantasy life; in other words, they define the world of film. Notable in Miss Deren's work (treated elsewhere in this book at more length) is its attention to dance rhythm and actual dance, sometimes only a sort of trance promenade. Traits of the trance promenade began appearing in Antonioni's films of the sixties in the persons of his wandering, sometimes brooding and confused heroines. Of course, there is a generic root for such bemused ladies (see *The Hollywood Hallucination*) in the old sensation-melodramas containing hypnotized, insane, and otherwise distraught or abused heroines: the Somnambules.

Their best-known prototype is the victim of attempted rape in *The Cabinet of Dr. Caligari*: a lady driven insane by a sexual trauma. The lady called "A" in the *Marienbad* film is a sophisticated parody of just such a heroine; so is (in the last scene) the film star parodied by Gloria Swanson in *Sunset Boulevard*. One should not overlook that the somnambulist heroine's erotic trauma is apt to be tinged with delusions of persecution and the more morbid sort of narcissism. Maya Deren always played her own heroines and always wore the absorbed look of intense inner contemplation, more or less agitated according to the occasion. In the commercial circuit, the climax of this type-heroine is seen in the heroine of *Juliet of the Spirits* (1965). Like deeply unhappy, deeply neurotic women, the artist himself is dominated by visionary and ecstatic experiences. Juliet—and Miss Deren's heroine too—are in line with Cocteau's prototypic poet as champions of the visionary life. Here is the crux of the avant-garde viewpoint. An "obsessed" visionariness may be not only a psychopathic or neurotic trait but also a medium of universal imaginative truth.

What has happened in recent years to the hollywood hallucination is that those desiring to create superior films (which make enough money to at least pay their way) have hit on an empiric formula to render the popular fantasy life in more select, enlightened, and adult terms, *but without dealing (as did Fellini's last two films) with the psychic technicality of "hallucination."* Suppose *all* life were considered a sort of mirage, an arbitrary world of hazard unbound from common sense and filled, even as science fiction, with implausible extravagance? This would be close to the Surrealist attitude toward reason and reality, even a deliberate vulgarization of it; in practice, it *has* to be vulgar and follow the established parody lines, although the parody is now more conscious.

That is to say, it is wilder, exploiting farce at whim (as in *The Knack*) and caricaturing everyday life as well as film genres themselves. As historic considerations of the movies' self-parody, the present book furnishes analyses of two important precursors: *Dead of Night* (1946) and *Sunset Boulevard* (1950). Exactly in this area of parody (fairly close to what we know in intellectual life as existential absurdity), the Nouvelle Vague sounded its most meaningful keynote, and with the mad film melodrama as partner, developed the sort of thing that has been climaxed by *The Tenth Victim*

14

(1966), truly an international film product. Since Pop Art became such a small rage, a general entente in the arts has been established with science fiction. Now in films, instead of Dracula, Frankenstein's monster or a hero of Edgar Allan Poe, we have the Superman secret agent and even (as in *Our Man Flint*) parodies of the same. Jean-Luc Godard's *Alphaville* offers the most sophisticated version of this hero, Lemmy Caution, a sort of robotized Humphrey Bogart, de-magnetized of charm and projected (like the occupant of a space capsule) into the future. Belmondo, in Godard's *Breathless*, set the parody note six years ago, but at least he retained charm.

The transformation of the mass hero who was the private-eye detective (say Bogart in *The Maltese Falcon*) to the mass hero who is secret agent and international spy (James Bond) is notable: it means a shift of tension from old-fashioned gangsterism and its antidote to the sub-rosa Superman of the Cold War and the ever-threatening future. In *The Tenth Victim*, a legalized group of men and women are potential killers and victims in a deadly "hunt" in which future society is supposed to have "rationally" channelized and limited man's lethal aggressive instinct. "Wars" have become obsolete. The film is strictly comic-strip fun despite its macabre theme; its broad brazen corniness and compulsive smirk are entirely in the new Pop spirit. As for the "art" commodity of Pop, it represents an insidious virus of the aesthetic corpus—and by "insidious" I mean nothing at all subtle.

Andy Warhol's impromptu films have been adopted by the current underground movement for two reasons: their impudent flouting of cinematic form except in fragments, and their embrace of taboo themes and atmospheres like homosexuality and drug-taking. Of course, for the last decade, homosexuality has not been nearly so taboo in commercial film as formerly. Lately, rather candid versions of it have come along although, like the movies' old-fashioned renderings of illicit love, it is characteristically associated with psychic disease and moral evil, or else appears frustrated or a subject for comedy or satire. My chapter here on the "underground" developments in avant-garde film deals with this subject in the special light of the style known as camp, which as a term has become common currency these days, largely owing to its built-in Pop flavor.

Camp, too, comes within the purview of the hollywood hallucination. It always did. Very recently it has been freed, and properly, from its original homosexual orientation and made to apply (as I duly assumed in the forties) to all manifestations of charade-sensibility in its parody forms. When I was very, very young, Mae West was an acknowledged camp. This was the chief reason why, as late as 1944, I compared her to a female impersonator. In the sophisticated circuit, Bette Davis has always been as much of a camp as a straight actress, and has proven it with her more recent films where her really pathetic moments (always caricatures of emotion) evoke hilarity rather than pitying sympathy. Her *Whatever Happened to Baby Jane?* and *Hush, Hush, Sweet Charlotte* were followed by Tallulah Bankhead's *Die, Die, My*

15

Darling. The comic-strip, or Pop, slant is unmistakable in all of them. Grisly melodrama had parodied itself by farcing the personality of declassé film stars (again, consider *Sunset Boulevard*).

In an era overshadowed by the means of total destruction and the awesome mechanics of space travel, on one hand, and the escape from it all through drugs, on the other, it is rather logical that art phenomena should produce fantasies of transcendence, immunization, and withdrawal and that, in turn, these should be vulgar. I ask all our observers to note the current cult for Batman, a hero of the defunct Hollywood "wonder" serials. The most omnipresent moral theme in the arts today is emotional neutralization, however deliberate and whether the instrument be dizzy fun or black improbable humor. There is one catch: neutralization itself is an uninviting state; hence the problem is how to withdraw, immunize, escape—*and also enjoy.* One solution is to let down all bars of reason and common sense, all canons of taste, and permit Old Man Id and his antique scandals to take over. In the movies, the chief alternative, unfortunately, is virtuous sobriety of a drearily documentary sort. Plain reassertions of human dignity, like that in *Nothing But a Man,* though quite commendable as such, are editorial prose, not creative fiction, and have little to do with the imagination and its art. Liberal moral pieties in such films become an excuse for a craft that is aesthetically drab, dispiritingly narrow and static. Only the stubborn strength of the documentary cult makes films like *Nothing But a Man* in any wise "successful." The theme is tactfully treated, the story well-acted, but that this film conceals a nightmare of far more unpleasant truths than any truth it reveals finds a key in the chapter I have titled "Hollywood as a Universal Church." This "church" is still another generic hallucination of which commercial films have made, and are making, hay while the sun of race-tension shines.

Film chic is a widespread opportunism, developing a strong vein in the independently supported film. It is not strange that "wildcat" movies should imitate each other and go against the commercial grain. Under pressure from the cliques, one must have a determined acumen to keep such an American film venture as *Hallelujah the Hills* (A. Mekas) distinct from Godard's more casual improvisations; the latter director has a big place in the sophisticated film circuit, the former a little place. In what way are they really alike? Both adopt old-fashioned popular formulas as themes for ingenious and detached, more or less tongue-in-cheek, comic variations. Actually the variations are unevenly amusing. Opinion in the world of film buffs, for instance, is apt to be divided over Godard's films, even between one Godard film and another. What Mekas' film obviously shares with all the Frenchman's films is a broad theoretic premise, which is easy to define regardless of how specific results are evaluated.

This premise is the hollywood hallucination *sans* firm story line, *sans* clear viewpoint, *sans* a basic intelligibility. Or one might put it like this: In the Nouvelle Vague as a stylistic entity, everything depends on correct points of reference to other films and film-types. Take Truffaut's *Shoot the Piano Player*, the *Marienbad* film, or Godard's *Alphaville*. In each case the complication, all the true substance, lies in the degree to which we may take as satirically relevant and amusing the variations upon well-known film-types. Truffaut's film is about a neurotic pianist, supposedly a serious musician. Yet to begin with, this musician is played by an actual café entertainer (Charles Aznavour) so that we have a "cute" French male type masqueraded as a serious musician. On top of that, according to the story, the musician is a withdrawal type so that his indifference causes a woman in love with him to commit suicide. I found this development (as performed) quite graceless and unconvincing. But the true point is: How convincing *was it meant to be*? The whole film strikes me as very charadish in mood. Like the obscurely tensed romanticism of *Last Year at Marienbad*, it is basically tongue-in-cheek, a kind of alienation-joke played coquettishly somewhere between straightface and farce. Truffaut's film, obliquely, is what *Alphaville* is brazenly: the farced tense and mood of comic-strip crudity.

By now it is fairly well known that the Nouvelle Vague openly admires certain American film styles and observation tells us how: with feelings that are partly sentimental and nostalgic, partly dry and satiric. This attitude has led, in practice, to the definitive style of the comic strip. Only the comic inflection that we find in the James Bond melodramas was needed to show the comic-strip fun at the heart of the enjoyment taken by millions of readers in far-fetched mystery and detective stories. It's the camp of reader-response. The way the originals were *read* becomes the way they are, nowadays, *filmed*. Thus film is a significant art of interpretation: a true "performing art." In 1944, I defined Disney's set of animal cavortings in *Fantasia* as a blackboard portrait of how great numbers of listeners to classical music actually hear it: vision rhythmically incarnates hearing. George Balanchine is perfectly legitimate and first-rate at this function but think how Disneyishly cute may be the rhythmic sense of a certain section of Balanchine's dance public!

In our era of absurdism and the failure-of-communication neurosis, we have to reckon with a universal impulse (cavalier among the arts) to interpret all serious things as somehow unserious. Let's face it: the generic sophisticated term for this substitute for seriousness is *camp*. But camp, in such a context, is relatively aesthetic. One strategic variant leads to the *consciously serious* enjoyment of life *only* through drugs: or, to put it somewhat more accurately, through *a sort of psychic autointoxication analogous to the effect of drugs*. Consider, in this light, the mood of *Last Year at Marienbad*. Doesn't it seem "high" in a consistently irresponsible way? We see many traces of the Surrealist manners that appeared in films by Cocteau, Buñuel, and Dali; that is, certain crucial steps in its action (aside from the game played in it) are given the look of sudden hallucination or virtual dream. The ingenious script by Robbe-Grillet and Resnais' fine control of style make the film clever, although (see later pages here) also, I think, a bad one.

17

The impact of an art, whether comic or serious or somewhere between, must depend upon the positive value of *what is involved*. "What, and how much, is at stake?" is a question every work of art or near-art must answer since the same question, consciously or unconsciously, is asked by every spectator, reader, or listener. The "smallness" of so much film art, held these days to be chic and amusing, is due to its deliberately electing to put very little at stake in terms of both form and content. Is not the point of *Marienbad's* satire that all its refined hocus-pocus about the resumption of an illicit love-affair is foolish and futile exactly because the initial erotic incident *had very little at stake*? We are not sure whether this hollowness is due to the nature of the particular incident or to the innate characters of the partici- pants. The film emerges as an elaborate dumbshow of which one thing, and only one thing, is perfectly certain: whatever the lucid truth, it scarcely matters to anyone concerned.

On the other hand, let us suppose this movie were an elegant, satiric re- telling (a sort of self-parody) of some other, more seriously meant film; anyway, a film that *believed* very much was at stake. Such a film might be Antonioni's *L'Avventura* or *La Notte*, both, I am certain, meant seriously as modern romances. Augment *L'Avventura's* ambiguous psychological mo- tives and the mystery of the girl's disappearance, introduce some fancy filming and contrive some Surrealist touches, and you would have something close to the style and substance of *Last Year at Marienbad*! Certain critical observers think that Antonioni is being too solemn; anyway, they find his later films boring. Evidently, these persons imagine he is not so involved in his concern for love as he pretends to be; or more relevantly, he has taken his neurotic lovers (who may be only too "true") more seriously than they de- serve.

But, to me, the *Marienbad* film is a much more convincing "criticism" of *La Notte* than any hostile review of it I have read. Which does not make Resnais' film the better one. Why not? Because, all cavilling critics to the contrary, *La Notte* has enough basis in actual human experience to justify Antonioni's special concern and his extensive method of portraying that con- cern. Both love and sex, in reality, are more important (unless I suffer from a severe hallucination of my own!) than they are assessed by *Marienbad*.

So far as one knows, drugs are not used by any of the characters in *Marien- bad*. But take note of the whole somnambulistic quality of the film, where no single action seems quite consciously motivated or controlled—much less what is called emotionally committed. Even the man's erotic pursuit has a sort of narcotic *haze* about it. Whatever really seems to happen is placed in doubt. This is not the same "doubt" as that in *Rashomon*! There, the con- tradictory ambiguity means an enrichment of reality, not an impoverish- ment. Instead of the unreal becoming real, as the Surrealists propose, instead of the irrational taking over as a mental program, an ambiguous and narrow borderline domain is created by *Marienbad's* author and director. Cocteau's worlds, as in *Orpheus* and *Beauty and the Beast* as well as *The Blood of a Poet*, were places where magic and the supernatural are positive and operative elements. They are not frauds or equivocations but the *true reality*; they enable men to realize themselves and to come into full possession of life's meanings.

On the contrary, to take another example, *8½* offers the story of a director's interesting failure to make a picture; it is a kind of clinical document in which the director's hallucinations are exempt from medical supervision only because he is not downright insane or incapacitated and remains "master of the set." The most absorbing aspect of *8½* is that it is an inside reportorial on the amusing way that directors of legendary extravagance and waywardness (say, Von Stroheim or Orson Welles) have dawdled, dreamed, and dandified through highly expensive films. Those of Welles and Von Stroheim could not be marketed without studio amputations. In fact these two men have been victimized by their own idiosyncratic headiness because waste itself is part of the commercial routine; it was just that Welles and Von Stroheim egotistically opposed the collectively sanctioned procedures of waste. However the popular prestige of the "film art" has advanced of late years. Yes, Fellini could market *his* "hollywood hallucination"! Again, in *Juliet of the Spirits*, which has a more orderly and straightforward plot than *8½*, the heroine's hallucinations are kept logically, though not formally, distinct from the reality around her. She is a harmless "sport" who, as the wife of a successful businessman, flirts with a variety of "cures" for marital unhappiness and its bad dreams before discovering her incurability; then, according to the story's end, she begins living contentedly in her own insulated world of fantasy. It may seem rude to say so, but whoever Juliet may be, I don't think she is her namesake, Giulietta Masina, or that the latter has experienced the catharsis supposed of her fictive impersonation. Miss Masina was so much better, truer, and more "alive," when acting the role of Cabiria.

Some of the following chapters are occupied with explaining that modern film, like other modern arts, is busy with the cults of making diurnal and environmental reality increasingly unreal, and substituting for it not a greater reality, but a pseudo-reality that is palpably fictitious, implausible, and preposterous. Hence: the overnight craze for Batman, James Bond's most potent rival. The fact that, as I write, Bond has other rivals (Harper and Morgan by name) is only a token that adult intellectuals as well as teenaged intellectuals tend to be ashamed when (unfortified by LSD or an equivalent) they consider what they have cultishly begun to admire. In the more respectable worlds of painting and sculpture, Pop Art was a great condescension, a desperate maneuver away from the uneasiness of living in a world of non-human abstractions—however big, bold, and hard. Such emergency measures as Pop are necessarily, even in their most popular forms, short-lived. Stamp-like, life-sized repetitions of the heads of movie heroines—I refer to Marilyn Monroe and Elizabeth Taylor—may tend to fill the gap for a while, but no stopgap (see my last chapter) is by its nature more than temporary. In order to be appreciated, all true Pop manifestations require—I shan't say LSD or marijuana, though both may come in handy—but rather the kind of suspension of critical alertness, the sabotage of consciousness, that drugs confer by changing the body's chemistry.

When Karl Marx invoked an "opium of the people," he was alluding to the faculty of the human mind to deceive itself, or let itself be deceived, with hallucinations. I argue that it makes little difference whether or not these hallucinations are technically "consciousness-expanding." Properly investigated, the effect of LSD (disregarding its incontestably bad results) will be found to "expand" only at the cost of corresponding shrinkage, no matter who the drug-taker is; that is, opening out in certain areas of sensation, perhaps even imagination, the organism will also contract and close upon itself in other areas of the mental and emotional constitution. In evaluating LSD and other "benign" drugs on the widest level, we should remember that the Orient has achieved very similar, and somewhat safer, results under the willed duress of sober physical and mental disciplines; that is, through daily practice of religions such as Yoga and Zen.

A great deal of our society is, or imagines itself, morally quarantined in the *No Exit* and *Exterminating Angel* complexes (for a discussion of the latter, see later pages). Partly this illusion is due to the paranoid effects of the Bomb's existence and the surviving legend of the Concentration Camps. In any case, the point seems to be that everyone must make (as if life were a movie melodrama) his "break for freedom." The Pop myths of the movies, very sophisticated or vulgar-sophisticated, oversimplify the human predicament by means of comic-strip fables and science-fiction jokes. While offering an LSD-type release from reality, the whole sophisticated Pop strategy minimizes the very value of the things whose deprivation has so much animated our discomfort and our protests. The depiction of sexual relations in · *Alphaville* and *The Tenth Victim* (both the latest in upper-class film Pop) is transparent parody of the coarsest comic-strip eroticism—stereotypes of very old-fashioned movies. Come hell or the fool future, in other words, BOY GETS GIRL. All such cuteness makes me a *little* or a *lot sick* according to how well my compensation mechanism happens to be working. I doubt that this reaction is peculiar to myself. An *Alphaville*, with its superior air of playful condescension toward its material, is fake intellectual satire for juvenile adults and adult juveniles. It is Glossy Entertainment: past, present, and future.

Yes, indeed! "Hollywood hallucinations" are still going strong. They will doubtless outlive the present writer just as they. have outlived the pleasure which they gave him when he was much more innocent, and younger. By the way: How old is mankind, according to the organic pattern of the individual human lifetime? I should say, offhand, that we live in an age when an adult can be prematurely young no less than a teen-ager prematurely old. Part of

20

the embarrassment of all our art cults is that one finds it hard to distinguish what is doddering from what is teeter-tottering. "What's New, Pussycat?" is such an obvious question to ask. "What's Old, Pussycat?" would be so much subtler.

Meanwhile, it seems only sensible and objective to notice that behind the evasions, pretensions, and high-flying ambiguities of fashionable film-making lies the glaring fact that, in the world of film, *cult* is to be distinguished from *art*, and *dream* from both. At the same time, since most of the films I shall discuss here start with the premise of being fiction, and thus "art," the dream and the cult can never be wholly isolated from the art: organically, they remain interrelated. Hence the classifications in this book represent emphases and not categories; viewpoints and not final definitions. I *never* suggested that the hollywood hallucination be swallowed without chewing.

21

I

THE ART

more or less fine

The Movies as a Fine Art

When I was in Paris in 1954, I was conducted through several floors (evidently a converted mansion) of the Cinémathèque Française, which then housed a great exhibition of cinema history that began with the earliest photographic studies of motion. Apparently in working order were many "Neolithic"-looking gadgets, and I was told that here were gathered—actually with all the style of a display of Oceanic culture—the most precious and significant filmic documents possessed by Europe, particularly by Italy. Though it was handicapped with crowding, this very condition promoted the air of departed parlor magic which the tortuous exhibit revived; frankly, I expressed my Surrealistic pleasure. Downstairs in the projection hall, I beheld two classic film curios dating from the second decade of this film-making century; their heroines were famed Italian beauties who persistently took fluid postures alternately smacking of pagan statues and the inmates of sanitariums in their less tranquil moments. The best acting I saw that evening was by a lady who, abused by the world and her lover, threw herself without ceremony on the floor of a café and gave a prodigiously prolonged exhibition of writhing. It was certainly, however polished, the agony of a fine art. But which fine art?

The cult of the movies is probably wider and more innately furious than many innocent movie-goers and readers of best-sellers (as well as insulated admirers of Picasso and Pollock) imagine. Right along with majestic retrospective shows of modern painters, the Museum of Modern Art—which includes a modest "cinémathèque" of its own—lately announced, without a quaver of self-consciousness, a retrospective of "The Films of Samuel Goldwyn," honoring a gentleman who may truly be said to have helped, in his way, to make Hollywood history, but who otherwise may be said to have meaningfully enriched the public domain only with malapropisms.

The clear fact about all locales and grades of film museums is that they belong to that category neatly and alertly labeled by André Malraux "The Museum Without Walls," which suggests itself as a univalent term for modern civilization. As a branch of Roman antiquity, the movie belles I saw at the

25

Cinémathèque properly mimicked the attitudes of statuary and properly evoked, *circa* 1911, the furors of Futurism with its urgent graphs of the havoc wrought, and the patterns made, by machines. The movies, a "living" pictorial record of moral and physical dynamics, may pretend to historical status, and while they are notably void of vast theory, no doubt exists as to their vast space, the camera eye and its privileges being such that, potentially, no privacy is sacred to them, whether human or that of remote nebulae. The cult of the movies is based mostly, therefore, on their history not as an art but as a humanly directed technological instrument. They have contributed to telltale missiles more than to fine art.

As museums of natural history are steadily becoming more artistic, instead of remaining like monumental antique shops made from taxidermists' premises, so art museums are becoming, *de rigueur,* more naturalistic—with only "token" walls such as the four sided movie screen has. After all, Hollywood, now a cult at the Museum of Modern Art, is more "natural history" than "art history." True, during the Museum's programs, one laughs and marvels at fashions in acting and dress, sometimes nostalgically or otherwise admiring them, but one does the same at the Museum of Natural History before fashions in protozoa, which can be fantastically funny. How serious, in one respect, life must have been struggling up from the slime and the ooze! But having come all this distance, when we see it ingeniously portrayed and enlarged by immaculate forms of tinted glass in a museum, we marvel and laugh indiscriminately.

Psychopathologists may say we laugh too much, and the laughter may be more sinister than we realize if it somehow soars to the historical level, where Marx observed (with stinging persuasiveness) that when history repeats itself—as happens in the cult programs of film museums—what was meant as tragic is apt to look farced. Of course, it is not that history has actually changed *within* the reel of antiquated film, except to deteriorate its clarity; it is that history has changed outside it, and the risible awe of seeing Sarah Bernhardt, acting Queen Elizabeth for the new art, prepare for a pratfall on a mountain of pillows and then duly land, has mainly to do with changes in stage fashions and the superior mechanics developed by acting, which now sustains a calisthenic grace it lacked in the last century. Everybody loves seeing Joan Crawford hoof the Charleston in a film of the twenties: she had—and still has—the know-how.

Yet the historical level of film art is like the historical level itself when considered as humanity's overall, persistent case: everything (but everything!) depends on the relative rightness of the gauge selected. The know-how of an art is never monolithic but fraught with divisive and decisive subtleties that stay outside history; outside, that is, the mere technical progress of an art medium. "Cinémathèques" more accurately might be known as "Smithsonian Institutes." A film showing on Broadway this week may avail the very flower of camera and laboratory processes, and we can estimate—if its leading actress is a decent spectacle—the precise degree to which the Delsarte manual of gestures has been outmoded. But this has nothing whatever to do with the aesthetics of fine art where, in a sense, an authentic tradition is never outmoded. If museums tell us anything, they tell us *this*.

Perhaps, of all arts, dance actually changes the least. American ballet dancers, for instance, have developed an athletic style (no matter how "Classic" the ballet) that distinguishes them nationally and inflects the somewhat modernized Classic figures they are taught even in new ballets. Thus, in the Museum of Modern Art's film auditorium, we giggle at the fastidious manoeuvres of Mlle. Geltzer of the Imperial Russian Ballet, performing with male partner a bacchanale for two, and there also we sit awestruck by a Hollywood test film of Pavlova, dancing "The Dying Swan" only for the camera's approval: the change of art manners corresponds to a shallow but positive shift in our sensibility. The aesthetic problem grows complex when the film art's documents are complete and unique in their own right. The cult for film documents, signified by the more or less mushrooming societies and clubs of the big cities, is sometimes frenzied and dominated by that comfortably smug, lazy exclusiveness of all clubs. "We are the elect; we are the nucleus, undeluded by passing fashions and true to an Alma Mater—D. W. Griffith, Erich von Stroheim, Robert Flaherty, the Russian School. Yes, the old ones had their faults—but their faults are as nothing to the faults of the new ones . . ."

The modern intelligence tends to overwhelm us, if it can, with "documentary evidence" of all kinds. But evidence of what? The rub is knowing the exact point one wishes to prove and what it is worth in a known scheme of values. Do the cults demonstrate only that the movies "have a past"?—are "respectable" like other fine arts? But everything in the world has a past! For time, going forward with Proustian virtuosity, seems to go backward simultaneously, and with disturbing élan. The major poems of Pound and Eliot are, outstandingly, résumés of aesthetic modes and religious fashions, and hence their paramount relevance to the Symbolist anthropology of Frazer's school. The *Cantos* and *The Waste Land* literally tend to be "museums without walls": culture as a pure, essentially timeless, spatial complex which may appear, like space in the film, as a labyrinth of openness.

Maybe this "agoraphobia" of the fine arts (ambivalently allied to that plain claustrophobia that sends hall-bedroom dwellers into movie palaces) is owing as much to the paranoia of the old—in pre-atomic and atomic days—as to the perennially expansive rebellion of the young. Minor conclaves of film cultists are apt to be voluntary concentration camps of self-congratulatory nostalgics. Poets, truly, are not so sociable as film cultists, but the effective imaginative trends of modern literature (Marianne Moore's poems are like exquisitely arranged shelves of antique and modern bric-a-brac) plainly point to an Alexandrianism of the art ethos. If Joyce's *Ulysses* could be dubbed an intensive capitalization of a day's culture, every Hollywood studio is to some degree an

27

Alexandria of technical devices and cultural fetishes working on speed-up daily schedules.

As Pound paradoxically emphasized, one must know "how to read" before one can enjoy the rich stores of a super-library. The *Cantos* at large are merely a more or less eloquent guide to a presumed Alexandrian library of twentieth-century culture. In such smart documentary exhibits as I saw fleetingly at the Cinémathèque Française, the collage principle of display bears witness to a basic filmic device formulated best by Sergei Eisenstein: *montage*. This is simply the formal juxtaposition of images which are not necessarily related in objective time and space but which, when placed with plastic symmetry together or sequentially on the screen, yield a specific feeling or idea. In this symbolism-tending optical device (with its mechanical relation to Surrealism) may be perceived, at once, the basic principle of the metaphor as well as of those elaborate metaphoric constellations distinguishing *The Waste Land* and the *Cantos*. One term for these constellations would be "cultural ellipses," for their object in both poems is to establish identity and congruence over large, shifting spans of time and space. The historical level of all the fine arts is where Pound directs our gaze—on to the *high* level—and if film history as the evolution of a fine art had its encyclopedic "Pound," that is where he would direct our gaze: telescoping Méliès' primitive Paris studio with all the superequipped playground-factories of Hollywood, Elstree, and Moscow.

Whether casual collage or calculated montage, the documentary method of museums is all right so long as one knows how to interpret it in correlation to internally aesthetic values; *i.e.*, "how to read" what is on view. The Surrealists, for their part in film history, quickly perceived the extraordinary faculties of the film camera for magical effects, and hence there arrrived the classic, small-cult repertory films, Dali-Bunuel's *Chien Andalou* and Cocteau's *Blood of a Poet*. The ever-growing and world-wide Experimental School has based itself four-square on these two films and, more recently, on Cocteau's Myth films. Well may the clever Cocteau, with subtle French directness and simplicity, have perceived that the straightest line between the film studio and the Museum Without Walls was precisely the "film magic" implied in the high legerdemain of classical myths. Orpheus' legend, in this sense, was a "natural" for Cocteau. The great disparity of aim between the more orthodox Surrealist line in *Chien Andalou* and that in *The Blood of a Poet* was that, in the latter, the creator had in mind an "Alexandrian" or capitalizing exploitation of the aesthetic experience itself: the artist copiously in relation to his "magic" as if contemplating the world in his own navel.

Rather than straightforward Surrealism, Cocteau's art here was a fantastic one, utilizing Neo-Classic symbolism as *The Cabinet of Dr. Caligari* had utilized Neo-Medieval symbolism (remember that Dr. Caligari's story turns out to be an asylum inmate's hallucination). *The Blood of a Poet* is simply a montage of fantastic image sequences in the service of a perfectly reasonable and completely stated idea. Cocteau knew enough to know that the artist's magic is no

28

mere private matter and that the explicit idea of a world "navel" existed in antiquity; if this navel was geographically identified, as antiquity identified it, it still symbolized the center of the world as the artist presumably symbolizes the center of the corpus of the human imagination. In the temple (or "museum") of art, the artist ritually (that is, symbolically) commits suicide as an individual only to be automatically reborn as an "Orpheus," the public laureate who expresses the sensibility of a great aesthetic collective. Of all arts, the movies are assumed—or at least hoped—to express the sensibility of a "great aesthetic collective": the "great," of course, defining *quantity* rather than *quality*. Cocteau's last Myth film, *Orpheus,* super-telescoped the chamber drama of his earlier "Experimental" *Blood of a Poet* by tracing, as it were, his own history as an avant-garde artist who became a member of the French Academy. At last, he might enter the Museum by the front, rather than the back, door—and that is what he did. The irony remains that the Museum has come to have only illusive walls; indeed, as such, it parallels *The Blood of a Poet's* last scene when his muse, an armless statue, solemnly proceeds out of the art salon, where he has shot himself, into the indefinably open space of the stars—the "stars," one might add, of the movies as well as of the universe.

It would be a fatal mistake to suppose that any actual museum, however inhibitively physical its walls, represents a highly selective process by which the vulgar and the pretentious have been adequately eliminated. One obstacle to filmic selectiveness is, of course, national pride and another is sectarian, or cult, pride. Independent hope for the film as a fine art lies mainly in what the term Experimental implies in the total cultural context: the conscious resort to basic studio and laboratory methods rather than conscious emulation of the broad, and quickly academicized, formulas achieved by the movies at their commercial best. So little is really artful in the "open space" of the cinema heavens, so much is merely chameleon! As widely acknowledged as this is by the cultivated public, even film museums fail to provide, with critical hint or selective example, vital and coherent standards by which to judge the merits of what they find worth preserving.

Maybe a museum (like a monastery) is a place in which to wander and muse rather than (like a university) to learn and judge. If that were quite true, there would be no quarrel as to whether the young, young movies deserve being rated as a fine art. But, in the first place, they have entered flexible museum walls without being taught as a fine art at colleges, which makes them a singular not to say also an embarrassing case among the arts. In some colleges, their history or their technique may be taught, yet that is hardly enough to rank them with music or painting, which have their own departments and their own schools. The movies have their "scholars," even (Heaven knows!) their "critics"—they have yet to create a recognized "school" of their own. They simply don't constitute a major academic subject even though they have imitated not only statues, but all the arts, for a very long time. There is no art, in fact, they have neglected to assimilate and ended, inevitably, by contaminating.

29

To be a true art, the movies must not only be "fine," they must be "great." Wrong in method, Hollywood is right in aim. But for greatness, no "montage" of documents, however major, will do; there must be major vision.

Today, scholars have created a Society of Cinematologists; yesterday, it did not exist. It may be a small but important step in the direction of prestige. The basic problem of how "fine" an art the movies can be remains a tantalizing problem. Characteristically post-facto thinkers never understand why the movies still have to *prove* themselves a fine art. These reasoners don't mean that Hollywood's own Academy is enough or that the movies are really an extension of Broadway's tacit institution, the Theater, but are like those who use the ontological argument for God's existence. If it were a question of "the movies" as only an advanced art of the nickelodeon!—but it is, they think, a matter of the motion picture as classifiable with painting or sculpture! Mainly, this is to rely on an insidious concept of antiquated date: the movies as a sort of painting and/or sculpture in motion. In brief, it is to assume Richard Wagner's grand synthesis of the arts transported to the film studios and ipso facto an accomplished fact (musical score by so-and-so). But because Wagner's reputedly "filmic" stage directions are followed today, at Bayreuth, by the projection of film during his operas, does not supply the necessary proof. Wagner still stands or falls on his music as the movies must stand or fall on their vision. Abstract formal values *can* be discerned consistently in the best movies of the past—*Dr. Caligari, Potemkin, Broken Blossoms*—but the worth of these "silent" films will remain relatively superficial till the art can develop an independent imagination which builds supremely important themes basically in terms of still and moving photography. Borrowing—as with such "literary epics" as *War and Peace*—is not enough. The "original script" must not be an adaptation but a creation that starts with nothing in the mind's eye but what Tolstoi started with; that is, a view of life *as life*, not as a "museum without," or with, "walls."

The "Underground": New Make-Up for the Avant-Garde

During the late fifties and early sixties—as the discussion of the dream structure of film in a following chapter will reveal—it was usual for me to espouse the experimental or avant-garde film *as an art*. In the article for which this is a replacement, I identified the aura of the experimentalists as "the *independent* art of the film." I am now forced to revise my formulations. As a sign of the time, Pop Art does just as well in print if it be called Pop; anyway, the noun, the substance of the thing, refers to an "art" which is a commodity; the art as such withers away even as one looks and leaves only the naked substantive, Pop. Nowadays, informed art criticism borrows from smart thinking about what is euphemistically known as *media*. Marshall McLuhan has adopted this term into the intellectual's vocabulary, chiefly with the arresting statement, "The medium is the message."

If this dogma be true, and wholly true of film, then film as a "medium" is a message, not an art; or it is a dream or what-have-you. Perhaps, as the Surrealist painter René Magritte has claimed of Pop, the film is theoretically another branch of "advertising art." Hustling, publicity-minded print about the newly christened Underground Film includes another label: Independent Film. Along with the New American Cinema, this trio of labels would supplant the previous duo: Experimental and Avant-garde. Theoretic objections to the two established terms are fairly obvious. "Experimental" carries an old stigma, implying both the unprofessional and the tentative, while "avant-garde" implies the exclusive: a snobbish minority. Small film makers these days wish to substitute the unprofessional for the professional and convert minority values to majority values. This is all very well, depending on *just what* the minority values are.

Certain critics have noted that the experimentalism of the older generation of the American avant-garde has turned from European stylization, chiefly the Surrealist trend, to much more obvious subject matter and to a deliber-

31

ately relaxed attention to craft, in which a free-wheeling private fantasy, utterly self-indulgent, simply throws *film form* onto the cutting room floor of the mind before even a single reel is shot; in brief, this informal yet cohesive "school" is a rival tendency of documentarism. What does it "document"? *Answer*: mostly the irresponsible impulses of not-so-extraordinary, but very ambitious, people.

An intellectual critic, Susan Sontag, has hailed the recent shift, in the case of the film *Flaming Creatures*, as providing the authentic article. This authentic article deserves to be viewed, thinks Miss Sontag, as beyond standards of form: a sort of ideal film-anarchy arising in sensibility. *Flaming Creatures* is a peep-hole into the film maker's private fantasies, which happen to be offbeat, erotic, violent, and notably messy. In one dimension, this sort of thing assuredly has its interest, and in that dimension it is indeed authentic; it even has moments of poetry, of filmic sensibility. Yet it is precisely the naïve adulation of a Susan Sontag, producing fashionable phrases smacking of existentialism, which both hides and distorts its true merits. In praising this film, Miss Sontag is a chic intellectual celebrating a quasi-creative variety of camp. Camp (see this book's introduction) is the quick-service version of absurdism that often dispenses with the humor which originally was inseparable from camp, and which made it an amusing parody. Once it becomes humorless (except for the sick joke which is fast becoming sick-unto-death), camp loses its main asset, *wit*, and turns itself into aggressive face-making by persons underprivileged in talent and intellect.

Ours is the day (alas!) of intellectual condescension, which rapidly leads to intellectual carelessness. At the moment of writing, a current literary fad is to discuss the death of God. To be sure, this is not so novel a subject as the journalistically minded pretend. Nevertheless it is treated as news—maybe it should be called "camp news." Over the passing years, a lot of brouhaha has been heard about the death of Art. Its death was the nihilistic idea first naughtily broached by the Dadaists and completely misunderstood (that is, distorted) when translated into journalese. The gods of Art have always died, and the gods of Religion, too. If dead gods maintained any fame, any lease on eternity, it was under the patronage of just such literary iconoclasts as the Dadaists and Surrealists. The latter were careful to choose their forebears from among artists; moreover in deifying principles such as the Irrational, they virtually made the Freudian Id a god, just as Nietzsche had re-deified Dionysos and Apollo.

An idolized precursor of the Surrealists, Isidore Ducasse, the "Comte de Lautréamont," fantasized personally dragging God from his "pedestal" and grinding him in the dirt, meanwhile deifying Mathematics as a trio of classical muses. We should not forget that the Christian God is one who invited humiliation, for in the form of his son Jesus, he allowed himself to be crucified. Does art, and the film art in particular, have its self-sacrificing Jesus Christ —its "camp" savior? It is an interesting speculation and very apt because of

32

The Art

Pre-World War I stage conventions reigned in Art Films until, with the appearance of *The Cabinet of Dr. Caligari,* modern aesthetics created a true plastic dynamism for the film frame. This classic of the museum repertory, made in 1920, heralded the best realizations of the Art Film, including the pioneer Surrealist works. Breaking free of both naturalism and hollow artificiality, *Caligari* identified the new visual sensibility with the exotic, the extravagant, and the dreamlike.

The Cabinet of Dr. Caligari   *Courtesy Gideon Bachmann*

Early Italian Film   *Courtesy Gideon Bachmann*

Orpheus (Jean Cocteau)   Courtesy Gideon Bachmann

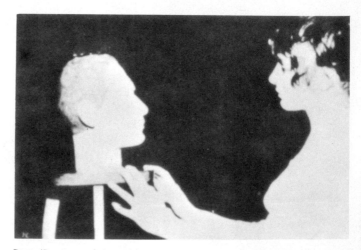

Narcissus (Willard Maas-Ben Moore)
Courtesy Cinema 16

Serenity (Markopoulos)
Courtesy Serenity Productions

Dom (Borowczyk-Lenica)   Courtesy "Film Quarterly"

Animated by Jean Cocteau with his early *The Blood of a Poet*, the museum image of the classic statue became a dynamo of the new Art style. This motif of the poet's classic role of establishing a new focus for great traditions has vied with Surrealist iconoclasm and Expressionist fantasy for ascendancy in avant-garde film-making. The Polish Surrealist film, *Dom*, parodied the statue motif with a clothes dummy's head. Commercial "art films" have succeeded only in superficializing and botching the artist's biographic legend, but recently an inspired Japanese film, *Rashomon*, made an unexpected contribution to the advanced cinema by rendering human experience in terms of the psychology of modern art.

Rashomon (Kurosawa)

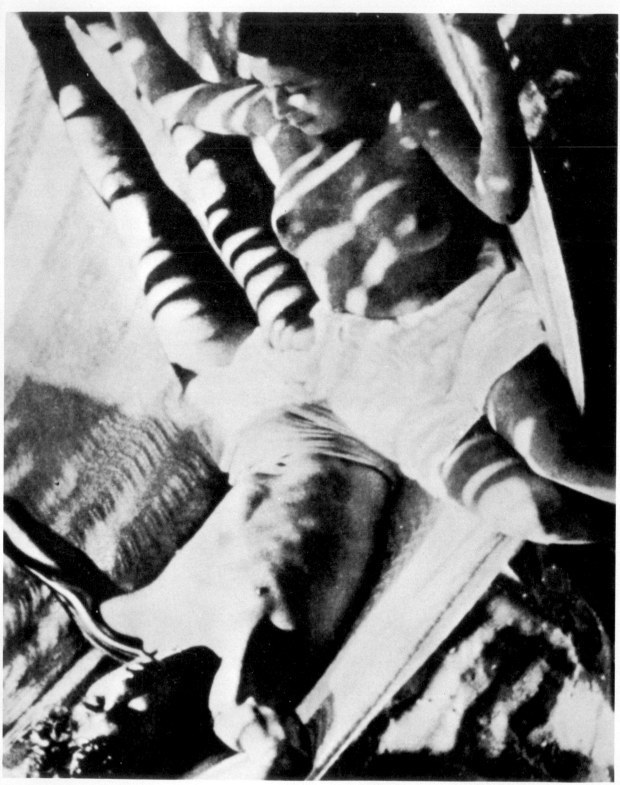

Time in the Sun (Eisenstein)

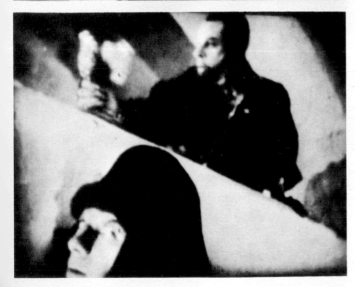

Ivan the Terrible (Eisenstein)   *Courtesy Janus Films*

Sergei Eisenstein was the only film artist
with the "eyewitness" psychology of the
camera who desired, and was able, to create
plastic compositions of the highest value.
When he essayed purely imaginative works,
he readily resorted to the devices of
chiaroscuro as a medium of poetry and
drama. The frames of film action on this
page might be based on details abstracted
from the variegated pattern of the couple in
the swing from his unfinished film, *Que Viva
Mexico!* Compare any whole frame on this
page with imaginary rectangles made by
a quarter or an eighth of the beautiful
composition opposite; also note, in all four
shots, the dynamic quality imparted by
diagonal thrusts.

On the Edge (Harrington)

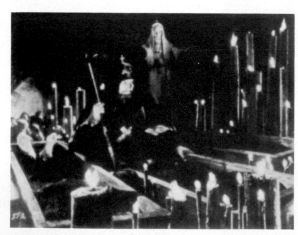

Ivan the Terrible (Eisenstein)

On these two pages are examples of the dramatic use of black-and-white that characterizes *Caligari* and Eisenstein's best films. How simply white-on-black and black-on-white are balanced (above) in the same frame, while the scene from *Ivan the Terrible* (left) is a little "sonata" of whites picked out of black. Opposite are two excellent results of the broad influence of modern painting on film: at top, concentrated shadow evokes an Expressionist gloom such as that in Munch's painting while, below it, concentrated light evokes a Post-Impressionist brilliance such as that in Bonnard's work.

The Seventh Seal (Ingmar Bergman)

Courtesy Janus Films

Wild Strawberries (Ingmar Bergman)

Courtesy Janus Films

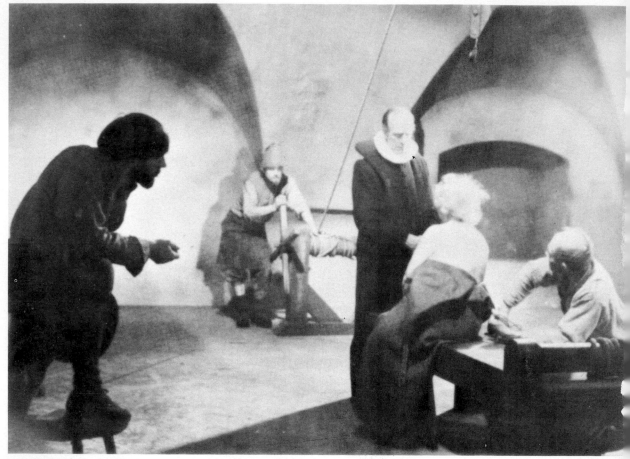

Day of Wrath (Dreyer)

Rembrandt: *The Toilet of Bathsheba*

The film shot reproduced above was as carefully composed as the great painting reproduced at left. Strikingly similar in their Baroque lighting, they offer but one eloquent proof of dramatizing the individual in space, whether (as here) he is an agent of concentrated light and dark, or (as elsewhere) he is abandoned to the risks of undefined space. This composition by Dreyer is a measure of how tightly the film actor can be made to fit the perfectly controlled manipulation of plastic values.

a film that has earned wide plaudits from radical film makers as well as from conservative critics: Pasolini's *The Gospel According to St. Matthew* (released in the United States in 1966). It is made in a sort of forthright, folksy, small-budget way, apparently with thorough honesty, without richly apparelled spectacle or other expensive technical costs. A few inspired touches of camera craft, quite filmic, "spot" it as its deliberately shabby story unwinds. The work is very far from being a masterpiece, and in terms of filmic method is no newer than the early Rossellini. In aesthetic quality, it veers from the bathos of the Salome episode (done "straight" like an illiterate Sunday School pageant) to some fine scenes between Jesus and the Apostles, walking windblown in the countryside or gathered in a circle while Jesus preaches and they listen.

This film's total effect is ragged and loosely impromptu: another feather in the cap of Dowdy Documentarism. One of the worst banes of the new "Underground" is that it makes no distinction whatever between simplicity of effect and failure of imagination. I should say that the desire to compensate for failure of imagination is the chief drive behind the organized Underground Film, whether "large" or "small," Pasolini's *Gospel* being a "large" example. Known in Italy as a Communist, this director provoked some startled wonder at his solemn Christian piety. However, if one has seen the Pasolini episode from the omnibus film, *Rogopag* (banned in Italy and not yet seen generally in the U. S.), one realizes that while engaged on the Gospel film, Pasolini decided to camp it up by doing a brief film making sarcastic fun of the Passion. This, indeed, is what might have been expected from a political radical. So why isn't the *Gospel* the deadpan version of the same "camp"? The only serious explanation of this film is the desire to present Jesus as the poor man's property—the man too poor, I mean, to have much imagination or much money. We have here an anti-de Mille (read anti-bourgeois) version of the religious myth. Yet Eisenstein, for instance, could have accomplished the same transfer from rich man to poor man, from bourgeoisie to peasantry, and still have produced a work of imaginative art.

Hence, contrary to rumor, the change of complexion in the experimental film field does not come from the direction of poetry at all. It does not explore fresh expressive means except in a very small range much disproportionate to the ambitious scale of some films. The new "style" is not *more radically* filmic but *more informally* filmic. That extraordinary life-giving juxtaposition of images, which in poetry was seen in the flowering of imagism, symbolism, and surrealism, has almost totally disappeared as a dominant filmic technique. A number of more talented Underground film makers (a few of whom may repudiate the label) have systematically created a fetishism of filmic mannerism, and treated vague, vague scenarios (possibly "cosmic" or "mythic" in idea) in terms of this mannerism; the results, though there are exceptions, are most unsatisfying and monotonous. One finds in the Underground little but immature obsession: obsession with certain subject matter (as in *Flaming*

33

Creatures, male transvestitism—not to be confused, by the way, with homosexuality) or obsession with certain psychic states close to euphoria (as in *The Flower Thief*). Euphoria is the quasi-aesthetic quality celebrated mainly in the magazine *Film Culture*. This quality is Janus-faced; originally, that is, it stems from youthful protest against all paternal institutions that repress; it is the stark face of outrage whose typical field now is the college camp(us). Regardless of its intellectual level, it expresses a spastic revolt of the deprived senses and the offended moral sense. Its other face is the Escape from It All: this can take any naïve orgiastic form. The Happening is its least demanding formula. Otherwise, all one has to do is to set a camera in front of it and let the fantasy-sense do a little warm spadework; sometimes the development of the fantasy-motif is left entirely to the actors.

One important factor exists that helps predetermine this new filmic complexion of the downgraded avant-garde or experimental film. In Shirley Clarke's film version of Jack Gelber's *The Connection*, it assumes a fairly coherent and dramatic form: drug-taking. Indeed this film is the key to the pseudo-aesthetic which inclines to follow sophisticated Pop psychology by wishing to substitute a chemical autonomy of the senses for an artistic autonomy. Recall that in *The Connection* a film is being made within the film, and eventually the film-maker, after quite a battering, is induced to drop his task and join the drug-takers.

The state of trance that—in Maya Deren's films preeminently—was a medium of the poetic imagination, has become, in the new filmic twist, a state of trance that conditions both the creative and responsive mechanisms of film making. It amounts to a primarily chemical, in preference to a primarily psychic, automatism and aims at a ready-made, self-persuaded audience. Maybe there is a marijuana school of film, an LSD school of film, mescaline and peyote schools of film. I do not imply that, necessarily, either director or actors really take drugs in order to make such films. In truth, all drugs represent a certain uncritical and imprecise psychic convention regarding form and its logics. It seems perfectly true, also, that there is an alcohol-response and an LSD-response, not only in the audience but likewise in the creative premises of the film-maker: a type-response to life. Maybe alcohol "accounts" for W. C. Fields' style of comedy. Yet the point must be that alcohol is not *all* that accounts for it, not what *decisively* accounts for it.

If only for reasons of empiric discretion, champions of the Underground Film prefer calling various type-euphorias "poetry." Yet such champions seem to imply that poetry is not something to be defined. Defining it, indicating its behavior and canons, would be much too academic. It wouldn't be "underground." And (between colleagues) it wouldn't be orthodox: wouldn't be laughing and unlaughing camp. It wouldn't (to relate the term historically) be *cricket*. Film audiences, of course, whether very special or very unspecial, always laugh—there are, as I imply elsewhere, cults of laughter, more or

34

less sophisticated, more or less perverse. In any case, laughter makes a ritual form of sheer nervous release. To cults, the whys and wherefores tend to be irrelevant. Cults *are*. So is "life," so is "revolt," so is the "Underground Film"! It's all one poetic camp; or it would be *if everyone were induced to take all camp at its face value.*

However, it is also true that wit is wit. And so is talent. They, too, *are*. The newer trends of the avant-garde film are notably unwitty or only unsuccessfully mimetic of wit. And their talent is remarkably hit-or-miss. Formal and intellectual film art, in a *Last Year at Marienbad*, is camped up, becomes sophisticated *blague*. Its existence seems to give everyone permission to be as silly as possible while *apparently* undertaking the serious. The comic strip, from Godard to Warhol, is the virtually avowed canon of the new "avant-garde" film's way of expressing *the human*. Analyze the comic strip and you have the perfect key to the latest competitor of James Bond; the key to the film buffs, gaga with admiration for Hollywood banality; the key to the camp-makers of what is called Fetich Footage (the most informal and fragmentary brand of Underground film).

In the subsequent chapter on the dream structure of experimental films, I indicate that the faults and inadequacies of the small independent film makers can be viewed as a variety of growing pains. This may seem, at this moment, rather idealistic of me, even uninformed. But, then, I am one who cannot accept the slick semi-success of what is roughly to be called Pop Film as anything but the result of a conspiracy among businessmen (including frustrated film makers). Pop, as a force in film, is simply another degradation of its art. As for camp, one must divide it into highbrow, middlebrow, and lowbrow. The *Marienbad* film is highbrow camp; certain Pop artists and the better Hollywood buffs propagate middlebrow camp; the movie *Harper* is, flatly, lowbrow camp. Those who have regard for life as a serious quantity must assert that, among these, the only object worth criticism *as an art* is that representing highbrow camp.

35

Rashomon as Modern Art

Rashomon, the Japanese film masterpiece, is a story about a double crime: rape and homicide (or possibly suicide). The time is the eighth century A.D. It is told in retrospect, and in successive layers, by the three participants, the dead warrior (through a mediumistic priestess), his raped wife, and a notorious bandit perhaps responsible for the warrior's death as well as for his wife's violation, and by a woodcutter who alleges himself to have witnessed, accidentally, the whole episode. The quality of the film narrative is so fine that an astonishingly unified effect emerges from the conflicting stories furnished by the three principals and (following the inquest) by the lone witness. The bandit and the woman have separately fled the scene of the crimes, where the woodcutter claims, at first, to have arrived only in time to find the warrior's corpse. Nominally, the film comes under the familiar heading of stories that reconstruct crimes. However, this story does not go much beyond the presentation of each person's testimony.

The woman claims to have killed her husband in an irresponsible fit of horror after the rape took place; her husband claims to have committed hari-kiri out of grief and humiliation; the bandit claims to have killed him in honorable combat; and the woodcutter confirms the bandit's story while picturing the conduct of all participants quite differently from the ways they respectively describe it. As no trial of either of the living participants is shown, and as no consequent action reveals anything conclusive as to the crime, the decision as to the actual truth of the whole affair falls to the spectator's option. Since technically the woodcutter is the only "objective" witness, he might seem the most reliable of the four testifiers. But his integrity is *not* beyond question; the version by the warrior's ghost has contradicted his version in an important detail—one inadvertently confirmed by the woodcutter's implicit admission (in an incident following the inquest) that he stole a dagger at the scene of the crime. The ghost has testified that he felt "someone" draw from his breast the dagger with which he alleges he committed hari-kiri.

Logically, if one's aim be to establish in theory the "legal" truth of the affair, the only obvious method is to correlate all the admissible facts of the action with the four persons involved in order to determine their relative integrity as individuals—a procedure complicated necessarily not merely by the given criminal status of one participant but by the fact that all but the woodcutter have willingly assumed guilt. A further difficulty, in general, is that nothing of the background of any character is given beyond what can be assumed from his visible behavior and his social status; for example, there is only the merest hint of something unusual in the journey of the warrior and his lady through the forest. Again, even from direct observation, we have to depend a great deal on these persons as seen through the eyes of each other. So, unless one be prejudiced for one sex or another, one social class or another, it seems almost impossible to make a really plausible choice of the truth-teller (if any). Are we to conclude, in this dilemma, that *Rashomon* amounts to no more than a trick piece, a conventional mystery melodrama, left hanging? My answer is *No*. There are several things about the movie which argue it as a unique and conscious art, the opposite of a puzzle; or at least, no more of a puzzle than those modern paintings of which a spectator may be heard to say: "But what is it? What is it supposed to mean?"

Perhaps more than one profane critic has wisecracked of a Picasso, a Dali, or an Ernst, that it demands, a posteriori, the method described by the police as "the reconstruction of the crime." My opinion is that the last thing required for the elucidation of *Rashomon's* mystery is something corresponding to a jury's verdict. Such a judgment, aesthetically speaking, is as inutile for appreciating the substance of this movie as for appreciating the art of Picasso. In *Rashomon*, there is no strategic effort to conceal any more than a modern painter's purpose is to conceal instead of reveal. The basic issue, in art, must always be *what* the creator desires to reveal. Of such a painting as Picasso's *Girl Before Mirror*, it may be said that it contains an "enigma." But this enigma is merely one specific aspect of the whole mystery of being, a particular insight into human consciousness in terms of the individual, and so has that complex poetry of which all profound art partakes. So with the enigma of *Rashomon*. This great Japanese film is a "mystery story" to the extent that existence itself is a mystery as conceived in the deepest psychological and aesthetic senses. As applied to a movie of this class, however, such a theory is certainly unfamiliar and therefore has to be explained.

Chagall with his levitated fantasy-world and childhood-symbols, Picasso with his creative analysis of psychological movements translated into pictorial vision—such painters set forth *nude* mysteries of human experience; each, in the static field of the painting, reveals multiple aspects of a single reality, whether literally or in symbols. *Rashomon*, as a time art, cinema, corresponds with multiple-image painting as a space art. The simplest rendering of time phases in an object within the unilateral space of a single picture is, of course, in Futurist painting, such as Balla's famous dog, ambling by the moving skirts of its owner; the dachshund's legs are portrayed multiply with a fanlike, flickering kind of image similar to images as seen in the old-fashioned "bioscope" movie

37

machine. The same dynamic principle was illustrated by Muybridge's original time-photography of a running horse, except that the register there was not instantaneous but successive; at least, the photographer had the cinematic idea of keeping pace with a running horse to show the pendulum-like span of its front and hind legs while its body seemed to stay in the same place (treadmill dynamics). Even in the contemporary movie camera, some movements may be so fast that one gets the sort of blur shown in Futurist images. The analogy of *Rashomon* with such procedures of stating physical movement is that, for the single action photographed, a complex action (or "episode") is substituted, and for the single viewpoint toward this action, multiple (and successive) viewpoints. The camera in this movie is actually trained four times on what theoretically is the same episode; if the results are different each time, it is because each time the camera represents the viewpoint of a different person; a viewpoint mainly different, of course, not because of the physical angle (the camera is never meant to substitute for subjective vision) but because of the psychological angle.

"Simultaneous montage" in cinema is the double exposure of two views so that multiple actions occur in a *unilateral space visually* while existing in *separate spaces literally* and possibly—as when a person and his visual recollection are superimposed on the same film-frame—also in separate times. A remarkable aspect of the method of depicting memory in *Rashomon* is its simplicity: each person, squatting in Japanese fashion as he testifies, squarely faces the camera and speaks; then, rather than simultaneous montage, a flashback takes place: the scene shifts wholly to the fatal spot in the forest. The police magistrate is never shown and no questions addressed to the witnesses are heard. When it is the dead man's turn to testify, the priestess performs the required rite, becomes possessed by his spirit, speaks in his voice, and the scene shifts back as in the other cases. Thus we receive the successive versions of the action with little intervention between them and with the minimum of "courtroom action."

Of course, there is a framing story, which retrospectively reveals the inquest itself. The action literally begins at the Rashomon Gate, a great ruin where the woodcutter and the priest, who has previously seen the woman and been present at the inquest, are sheltered during a rainstorm; joined by a tramp, these two gradually reveal everything that has taken place according to the several versions. What is important is the inherent value of the way the technique of the flashback has been variously used. The separate stories are equally straightforward, equally forceful; no matter which version is being related, his own or another's, every participant behaves with the same conviction. As a result (it was certainly this spectator's experience) one is compelled to believe each story implicitly as it unfolds, and oddly none seems to cancel another out. Therefore it would be only from the policeman's viewpoint of wanting to pin guilt on one of the persons that, ultimately, any obligation would be felt to sift the conflicting evidence and render a formal verdict. Despite the incidental category of its

38

form, *Rashomon* as a work of art naturally seems to call for a response having nothing to do with a courtroom.

Of an event less significant, less stark and rudimentary in terms of human behavior, the technical question of "the truth" might prove insistent enough to embarrass one's judgment. The inevitable impulse, at first sight, is to speculate on which of those who claim guilt is really guilty of the warrior's death. But whatever conclusion be tentatively reached, what eventually slips back into the spectator's mind and possesses it, is the traumatic violence of the basic pattern: that violence which is the heart of the enigma. The civilization of this medieval period is turned topsy-turvy by the bandit's strategy, in which he tricks the man, ties him up, and forces him to witness his wife's violation. It is only from this point forward that the stories differ: the woman's reaction to the bandit's assault, the husband's behavior after being freed from his bonds— everything is disputed by one version or another. But is not the heart of the confusion *within the event itself?* Is this happening not one so frightfully destructive of human poise and ethical custom that it breeds its own ambiguity, and that this ambiguity infects the minds of these people?

All the participants are suffering from shock: the warrior's agonized ghost, his hysterical wife, the bandit, when caught, seized with mad bravado. Unexpectedly—for the paths of the couple and the bandit have crossed purely by accident—three lives have been irretrievably altered after being reduced to the most primitive condition conceivable. Two men (in a manner in which, at best, etiquette has only a vestigial role) have risked death for the possession of a woman. Basically, it is a pattern that was born with the beginnings of mankind. Such an event, in civilized times of high culture, would of itself contain something opaque and even incredible. What matters morally is not how, from moment to moment, the affair was played out by its actors but that it should have been played *at all*. The illicit impulse springing up in the bandit's breast as the lady's long veil blows aside, is so violent that its consequences attack the sense of reality at its moral root. Regardless of what literally took place in the forest's depths that mild summer day, each participant is justified in reconstructing it in a manner to redeem the prestige of the moral sense, which, consciously or not, is a civilized person's most precious possession. It should be emphasized that it is the Japanese people who are involved, and that to them honor is of peculiarly paramount value; even the bandit is quick to seize the opportunity to maintain—truthfully or not—that he behaved like a man of caste rather than an outlaw; he has testified that following the rape (to which, he says, the woman yielded willingly) he untied the husband and worsted him in fair swordplay.

Hence, a psychologically unilateral, indisputable perspective exists in which the tragic episode can be viewed *by the spectator:* a perspective contrary to that in which one of the persons appears technically guilty of the warrior's death. This perspective is simply the catastrophe as a single movement which temporarily annihilated the moral reality on which civilized human consciousness is based. The "legal" or objective reality of the affair (what might be called its *statistics*) is exactly what cannot be recovered because the physical episode, as human action, has been *self-annihilating*. Of course, then, it might be claimed that the woodcutter, not being involved except as a spectator, is a disinterested witness of the episode, and accordingly his story that the three actors in the tragedy really played a grim farce, in which two cowards were the heroes and a shrew the heroine, is the correct version. But the opening scene of the framing story makes it plain that the woodcutter's mind is in a state similar to that of the participants themselves; indeed, he is evidently dismayed and apparently by the fact that all their testimony belies what he proceeds to reveal to the priest and the tramp as "the truth." However, as the shocked witness of such a debacle of the social order—in any case a victory of evil over good—this peasant may have withheld his testimony out of superstitious timidity. If, in fact, he saw all that took place, then the added confusion that the participants contradict each other may raise bewilderment in his simple mind—may even tempt him to exploit his subconscious envy and resentment against his betters by imagining their behavior as disgraceful and ludicrous. It seems within *Rashomon's* subtle pattern to suggest that even a simple, distinterested witness should be drawn psychologically into the chaos of this incident; after all, there is no proof that he did not invent his own account in competition with the others'. This assumption would lend credit to the conclusion that the real function of each witness's story is to salvage his own sense of reality, however close his version to the event as it took place. Perhaps it would be accurate to add that the facts themselves have no true legal status since each witness is forced to draw on his subjective imagination rather than on his capacity to observe. In this case, each is in the position of the proto-artist, who uses reality only as a crude norm; the sense of invention enters *into* reality. On the other hand, there is the literal truth of the denouement, the climax of the framing story, in which the woodcutter adopts a foundling baby who has been left in the Gate's interior. The relation of this incident to the story proper strikes me as the most problematical element of all, if only because the film would have remained intact without it.

Morally, of course, this incident functions as a reinstatement of human values in the sense of good. But the specifically religious view that humanity has hopelessly degraded itself in the forest episode (the view represented by the priest) is more external than essential to the whole conception. The priest thinks in terms equivalent, logically, to the law's terms: truth or falsehood. Since some lying is self-evident, the sin of concealment is added to crime; *i.e.*, concealment of the truth, not of the crime, for all profess crime. Ironically enough, *confession* has become a sin. What seems significant to the whole is the collective nature of the liars: they literally outnumber the truth-teller (whichever he may be). The "sin" involved has gone beyond individual performance and exists objectively as would a natural cataclysm such as a volcanic eruption. That each participant assumes guilt, including the dead man, reveals the com-

40

prehensiveness and irresistibility of the disorder. A lie, then, actually becomes the symbol of the operation by which these people mutually regain their moral identities. These identities having been destroyed as though by an objective force beyond anyone's control, any means seems fair to regain them. Since, however, they cannot separate themselves from the sense of *tragedy,* they prefer to be tragedy's heroes—its animating will rather than its passive objects. But why should the three tragedies seem as one?

To revert to our analogy with the visual media of painting and still photography, the plastic reality with which we have to deal in *Rashomon* is multiform rather than uniform. Within one span of time-and-space, reality (the episode in the forest) has been disintegrated. While the witnesses' stories accomplish its reintegration, they do not do so in terms of the *physically unilateral* except in the final aesthetic sense in which the totality of a work exists all at once in a spectator's mind. The analogy is complex, but literally it is with the Futuristic image of the walking dog; like this image, the total image of *Rashomon* varies only in detail and degree. There is no variation on the background and origin of the tragedy; no contradiction as to the main physical patterns of the rape and the death of the warrior by a blade wound. So the main visual aspect is held firmly, unilaterally, in place. Another image of Futurist painting renders the angles of air displacement caused by the nose of a racing auto. Such "displacements" exist in *Rashomon* severally in the respective accounts of a physical action deriving from one main impetus: the desire to possess a woman.

The total psychological space in this movie, because of its complexity, is rendered in literal time as is music. A similar psychological space is rendered *simultaneously* in Picasso's *Girl Before Mirror* by the device of the mirror as well as by the double image of profile-and-fullface on the girl. Her moonlike face has a symbolic integralness as different "phases" of the same person; that is, her fullface denotes her personality as it confronts the world and her profile her personality as it confronts itself: the mirror image in which the fullface character of her aspect is diminished. To Meyer Schapiro we owe a basic observation as to this painting: it plays specifically on the body-image which each individual has of himself and others, and which is distinct from the anatomical image peculiarly available to photography. The mirror image in Picasso's work thus asserts a psychological datum parallel with the dominantly subjective testimony of each witness in *Rashomon's* tragedy. The mirror of the movie screen is like the mirror in the painting as telescoped within the image of the total painting; successively, we see people as they think of themselves and as they are to others; for example, at one point during the woman's story, the camera substitutes for the viewpoint of her husband toward whom she lifts a dagger: we see her as conceived by herself but also as she would have been in her husband's eyes. In revealing, with such expressiveness and conviction, what novels have often revealed through first-person narratives or the interior monologue, the film necessarily emphasizes its *visual* significance. The sum of these narratives in *Rashomon* rests on the elements of the tragedy in which all agree:

41

one raped, one was raped, one killed, one was killed. The "variations" are accountable through something which I would place parallel with Schapiro's body-image concept: the *psychic image* that would apply especially to the memory of a past event in which the body-image is charged with maintaining, above all, its moral integrity, its ideal dignity. In a sense, Picasso's girl reconstructs and synthesizes her outer self-division within the depths of the mirror; so in the depths of each person's memory, in *Rashomon,* is recreated the image of what took place far away in the forest as consistent with his ideal image of himself.

In modern times, the human personality—as outstandingly demonstrated in the tragi-comedies of Pirandello—is easily divided against itself. But what makes a technically schizophrenic situation important and dramatically interesting is, paradoxically, the individual's sense of his former or possible unity, for without this sense he would not struggle morally against division: he would be satisfied to be "more than one person." In analytical cubism, we have a pictorial style expressing an ironic situation within the human individual's total physique, including his clothes; we do not perceive, within an individual portrayed by Picasso in this manner, a moral "split" or psychological "confusion"; rather we see the subject's phenomenal appearance portrayed formalistically in terms of its internal or "depth" elements, its overlaid facets, or complex layers of being, which—though presumably not meant to signify a conflict in the personality—correspond logically, nevertheless, to the moral dialectic within all consciousness (subjective/objective, personal/social, and so on). The same logical correspondence is seen even more plainly in the anatomical dialectic of Tchelitchew's recent paintings, where the separate inner systems are seen in labyrinthine relation to the skin-surface. Indeed, man as an internal labyrinth is common to diverse styles of modern painting, all such styles necessarily implying, as human statements, the sometimes bewildering complexity of man's spiritual being. Great beauty is justifiably found in such aesthetic forms, which indirectly symbolize an ultimate mystery: that *human* mystery to which *Rashomon* so eloquently testifies in its own way and which comprises the transition from birth to death, from the organic to the inorganic, which is the individual's necessary material fate.

Against the awareness of his material fate, the individual erects many defenses: art, pleasure, ethics, God, religion, immortality—ideas, sensations, and acts whose continuity in him are preserved by constant cultivation, periodic renewal, unconscious "testimony." These constitute his moral identity in the social order. In them resides the essence of his being, the law of his contentment (such as it be), and his rational ability to function from hour to hour. In the lives of the persons of *Rashomon,* where this objective order prevailed, utter chaos was suddenly injected. Each person was shaken out of himself, became part of that blind flux which joins the intuition of the suspense-before-birth with that of the suspense-before-death and whose name is terror. This was largely because of the tragedy's physical violence, which temporarily vanquished human reason. If we look at the terror of war as depicted in Picasso's

Guernica, we observe a social cataclysm of which the forest episode in *Rashomon* is a microcosm. Curiously enough, *Guernica* happens to be divided vertically into four main sections, or panels, which Picasso has subtly unified by overlapping certain formal elements. Thus, while the great massacre is of course highly simplified here in visual terms, it is moreover synthesized by means of four stages or views. As wrenched by violence as are the individual forms, they congregate, so to speak, to make order out of confusion. Though Picasso was not recomposing from memory, he might have been; in any case, the drive of art is toward formal order and the individuals in *Rashomon,* as proto-artists, have this same drive. As gradually accumulated, the sum total of *Rashomon* constitutes a *time mural* whose unity lies in the fact that, however different are the imaginations of the four witnesses, whatever harsh vibrations their mutual contradictions set up, the general design (as the film-makers have molded it) remains and dominates the work's final aspect of great beauty and great truth.

The Film Sense and the Painting Sense

There has always been commerce, more or less conscious, between painting and the film. When first photography was invented, the aim was to duplicate the aesthetic effect of painting. Then when the concept of motion was introduced and the movies arrived, the aim deviated to a quest for realities on the one hand and magical fantasy (such as stage illusions) on the other. The very nature of the movies as visible animation suggested adventure rather than formal control, sheer excitement rather than aesthetic emotion. Commercial films have continued to obey this suggestion while serious tendencies in the motion picture have developed the plastic and dynamic senses of the medium in accordance with aesthetic principles. If some enlightened persons are disinclined to consider the movies an "art," it is not only because movies reproduce images mechanically but also because they so seldom, in their instantaneous imagery, suggest the calculated and controlled design of painting.

Because objects in the real world, moving or animate, may be faithfully recorded by the film camera does not produce on the screen a dynamic effect except in the most elementary sense, or a plastic effect except in the sense that the framing may casually create a rough composition. To attain consistent and satisfying plastic and dynamic effects, the camera must be used consciously, selectively and inventively in regard to *what* it photographs and *how* this is photographed. A rudimentary plastic design such as Mickey Mouse or a highly complex one such as Bosch's *Garden of Delight* are "stills," inanimate subjects, which the movie camera—as we have seen—can approach as raw material, just as though they were life itself. By thinking of the movie camera as an independent aesthetic agent, distinct from the art work it represents, we can observe its function as an *animator* in a rather strict sense.

Griffith, in his film *Intolerance,* approached his huge panoramic Babylon the way the camera may approach, as it did lately in *The Titan,* the great structures of human anatomy that Michelangelo placed on the Sistine wall in *The Last Judgment*. Both those photographed objects were created plastically before the camera faced them, yet the camera tends to "dramatize" them as

44

A "Art is the language of emotion," S. K. Langer

though it were an individual spectator noting them in ensemble and then in detail, or vice versa. And just as a kind of narrative is involved with Griffith's Babylon, which was only an immense stage set, so a kind of narrative is involved with the single plastic entity that is Michelangelo's mural. Since the cinema as a form is literally a series of pictures, it is automatically adapted to show narratives, or action in quantitative time. Therefore, it may move before Bosch's congeries of images as though they were a medieval passion play; similarly, it may pass before Giotto's murals relating Christ's story in the Arena Chapel and reconstruct the *Massacre of the Innocents* as though it were live action.

In the recent *Leonardo da Vinci,* the artist's analytical drawings of birds in flight were animated in the orthodox "Disney" fashion. This cannot be done with other authentic works without a deal of faking, but an approximation of it has been employed twice in the use of dance-drawings by Toulouse-Lautrec. In *Pictura,* two stages of a kick in drawings of the same dancer are repeated over and over rapidly to give the standard animated effect, while in *Moulin Rouge* a sequence of Lautrec's dancehall figures are run swiftly before the eye and intercut to produce the *impression* of real action in the famous café. Eisenstein, in his *October,* animated three separate sculptures of lions, recumbent to rampant, with distinct comic success.

Animating a given plastic composition by a great artist may strike one as not only a vulgar but also a criminally absurd idea. Yet in *The Titan,* for an outstanding example, an effect of much subtlety was obtained by passing the camera at close range around the somnolent figures Michelangelo placed before the Medici tombs. This might be called a *controlled spectatorship* in which the photographic values of black and white within the quadrangular two-dimensional frame contributed an "interpretive" rendering of the allegoric sculptures. Signally, too, with the *Bacchus,* the movie camera "narrated" a way-of-looking that was a way-of-feeling, the rectangularly isolated views achieving a special plastic effect that would not have been thus precise without the camera's use.

The Titan's interpretation of the Michelangelo sculptures, bringing three-dimensional works to the movie screen *as though* they were elements of flat composition, refers to an important aspect of the art of the film. This, as Eisenstein has voluminously shown, is the conception of film not as a representation of a three-dimensional world in terms that (like those of sculpture and bas-relief) remind us literally of the third dimension, but rather in terms that remind us literally of the two dimensions of painting. Eisenstein's completed first part of *Ivan the Terrible* earned unfavorable criticism as "static" because it clung to single plastic compositions for such protracted periods. Analysis of these compositions show the lasting effects on Eisenstein of his early experience as designer of abstract-geometric stage sets. Actual motifs of Kandinsky's imagery are discoverable in *Ivan.*

In his unfinished *Que Viva Mexico!* Eisenstein constantly bore testimony of

45

his debt to painting by projecting screen shots that were virtually "stills," carefully composed with plastic values in mind. Essential to these beautiful shots were the two-dimensional feeling of surface and, of course, the rectangular screen. The latter was always an element of the movies' artistic function and was apt to operate best in the pre-talkie era since in the talkies the film often tends merely to photograph actors speaking, and to follow them about as though they were on a theater stage. This last, indeed, is specifically what Alfred Hitchcock did in *Rope*, thereby destroying all opportunities for true cinematic composition in the "still" sense.

If one film trend animates painting, as we have noted, another de-animates life into the still terms of painting insofar as its aim is plastic two-dimensional composition as a unit in its spatial-temporal art. One may define the film as a plastic, two-dimensional composition which animates itself in a series of mutations, totally replacing one composition at a certain point with another. *Style* is the element expected to unify so many different compositions. The film, then, is a fused art of time and space. So, in a distinct capacity, is the theatre. So are, in other respects, mural painting and the "narrative pictures" of the Renaissance. Technical animation of the popular cartoon kind, when applied approximately to works such as the sequence of Lautrec's Moulin Rouge drawings, actually treats plastic images of dancers *as though* they were live performers and not as the central forms in works of a two-dimensional art. Among other things, what such animation accomplishes is a "flashback" impression of the dynamic elements which temporally went into the making of the work.

The technique of the film has allowed us to see, as one continuous movement, a plant growing from seeds below ground to sprouts and leaves above ground (*Farrebique*) and a rose developing from bud to blossom. Analogous to this visual intensification of an objective dynamic process is what the film may do with the progress of a painting's creation. In a documentary on Matisse, we are shown how the artist developed his conception of a head in a series of sketches from a quasi-naturalistic version to the final form. This was done by superimposing the finished sketches transparently so that an illusion of organic evolution was obtained. Mickey Mouse as well as Lautrec's dancers seem to turn into organic beings before our eyes. But in the case of Matisse's head the element of *mutation* is added; in fact, the animation resides strictly in this element.

The painting-in-motion genre of the film art has been long in existence. The pioneer Oskar Fischinger animated pure-abstract forms in a kind of ballet to music and recently much work of this kind (notably by Norman McLaren and the Whitney brothers) has been done in the experimental-film field. Of special interest is a little *tour-de-force* by Thomas Bouchard in his documentary on Fernand Léger. The distinct formal units of one painting, having been analyzed, were cut out, painted as in the work, and then, by way of Léger's own hand, placed piece by piece in a position so as to reconstitute the picture. Previously Léger has been shown drawing directly from nature so that the *collage* operation of the film, especially since photographed from directly above, has an air of magic.

A distinctive aspect of the animated cartoons is the absence of motion in the background in contrast with the cavorting figure in front. We sense the background simply as a drawing. It is likewise with the blank ground of drawing paper or canvas on which the designs of artists, through the film, acquire the magic attribute of "organic growth." Yet this blank "background" is not a void but a physical plane surface limited by edges; in this sense, the sides of the paper are equivalent to the sides of a film frame as projected. In the old days when animation was becoming popular, a clown used to be born illusorily from an ink bottle in lines of ink, and the humor of it was his dependence on his creator for things to use, a world to live in, and sometimes even ground to stand on. This was a comic version of the myth of divine creation and like all myths its elements reverberate in time and space. Thus we saw one of the ingenious UPA cartoons, *Christopher Crumpet,* in which properties and backgrounds are created as well as animated before our eyes, appearing and disappearing as necessary. Here, in a pointed sense, the world is shown as *man*-created, and this is what, in our urban civilization, the visible world often is.

A great problem of our time is the world which group and individual find to live in and their capacity to change this world according to needs and desires or passively to be changed by it. Imaginative workers in the experimental-film field have contributed insights into this human problem by ingenious exploitation of the film's aesthetic possibilities. The classic avant-garde film, Cocteau's *Blood of a Poet,* has been most influential in this respect. Cocteau created a basic odyssey: that of the human creator. The narrative fluidity of his film was oriented to definite stages so that the mutating image of the hero becomes a spectator of closed interiors like small stage sets, visible to him only through a keyhole. The final set, the largest and equivalent to a small theater, opens into an exterior characterized as cosmic space, where the hero's destiny, and implicitly that of all artists, is finally transmuted into glory by the artistic instinct.

Maya Deren is a film-maker who has profited richly by Cocteau's example. The chief theme of some half-dozen films by her is the odyssey of an individual always engaged in something like an obstacle race and behaving like a somnambulist or one moving through an actual dream. The rhythms are often choreographic and dreamlike, the visual overtones labyrinthine. When, in Miss Deren's *Study in Choreography for Camera,* a dancer begins his movement in a wood, continues it without the least interruption as the scene shifts to a private interior, then to a hall in a museum, then to another interior and back to the wood, reaching his climax with a triumphant sense of dance-flow, we have an active, self-contained figure seen before a background whose seemingly arbitrary and sudden mutations are independent of his movements and of which he seems quite unaware. This is a parable of the individual's integrity in a changeable environment. But what gives this dancer his implicit confidence in the continuity of the solid ground he requires for his steps? It is, I think, the confidence of the artist who essentially creates his own space by establishing some plastic or dynamic rhythm in time and following it through consistently. The "ground" he assumes is the basic, limited ground which every artist uses.

Evident in Miss Deren's film fantasies (and in conspicuous ones by Sidney Peterson, Curtis Harrington, and Kenneth Anger) is the creation of an imaginary visual world in which tension is supplied by the protagonist's effort at control and equilibrium within it. We see the same basic theme in the adventures of the animated-cartoon characters. The fabulous feats of UPA's short-sighted "Mr. Magoo," blissfully unconscious of his perils, is a distinct example of the special tension I mean. What is implied is the very aesthetic of the film, which is the continual replacement of imagery (mutation of the whole composition) while sustaining intact certain *pivotal* elements of substance, form and style.

John Huston's *Moulin Rouge* and Carl Dreyer's *Day of Wrath* are two films that have profited from the sense of painting; scene by scene, the latter consciously aimed at a Rembrandt-like chiaroscuro. In the nonchalant assumption of the usual commercial film that the only necessary formal element is *plot* and that merely conventional "framing" and clear photography are required for plastic values, we find the reason for the vulgar journalistic look and formlessness of standard movie products.

The frantic drive of Hollywood cameras to "eat up" space on their recurrent "trips to the moon" directly reflects the general Hollywood conception of space as a jungle, a *chaos,* whether void or occupied. Art, on the contrary, is produced by the controlling principles of a *cosmos,* which underlies all casual aspects of confusion and variety and represents destiny as opposed to chance, form as opposed to formlessness. To achieve a meaningful art, the film has to invent not only in terms of its own exclusive nature but also in terms of the formal law which it shares with painting. Documentaries and newsreels can passively resign themselves to reporting. Creative films must obey a synthesis of aesthetic principles that have existed since the origin of the visual arts. A scrutiny of the animating devices may inspire us to perceive how movement can be formally initiated and artistically controlled within a given space.

The Artist Portrayed and Betrayed

Does "the" artist exist? The cult of the artist's bohemianism, the myth of his genius allied to his abnormalcy and extremism, the statistics, often so misleadingly publicized, of his strivings, his life and his death, all have enormous currency and have crystallized here and there into popular stereotypes. That an artist should be antisocial is no surprise to people who believe that genius is haughty and harsh, if not ashamed of its own excesses and strange look and thus "shy." Painters have always enlisted unusual public interest because they provide such concrete "imitations" of life. They are empowered, above all, to flatter the individual—to give him a lovely portrait of himself that nature has perhaps overlooked or sabotaged. Certainly this is part of the charm of seeing Toulouse-Lautrec, a dwarf, yearning after women whom he paints: the crippled genius paying his homage to beauty and perfection beyond his reach, alien to his own image. It is of a very sad, but perhaps symbolic, significance that in Huston's *Moulin Rouge,* the most ambitious fictional "portrait of an artist" since Korda's *Rembrandt,* Toulouse-Lautrec should be given not merely a stuffed-suit incarnation of his known image, but also a forged Lautrec hand drawing his work and a forged Lautrec portrait of a lady: Marcel Vertès was the stand-in for these details of performance. Though we had, in *Moulin Rouge,* some unusually good "atmosphere," including the Technicolor, we also had an emphatic token of the spurious conviction of the movies that anything in the shape of a photograph is triumphantly persuasive of truth.

Lautrec's legs are the disguised thighs of an actor with normal-sized legs. When Lautrec is seen reclining, the visible trouser legs are stuffed. Mr. Ferrer was well instructed in the stances, moving and inert, of someone with short, weak legs, who usually has to look skyward to see things. The Barnum and Bailey angle of the artistic genius is here given a naturalistic shaking-up. And we are supposed to be grateful for a milieu of scientific conscientiousness which shows us so faithfully a famous painter in his habit as he lived. But the actual truth is that all the clinging-to-fact paraphernalia of modern modes in fiction serves only to emphasize the fudge at the heart of such matters. A bitter and

49

beautiful story, with an appropriate image of the man, could be made of Tou-louse-Lautrec's life. What we have is a politely iced dose of sentimentalized "realism," itself only a frosting over of any responsible image of the truth. The convention of a sacred/profane eroticism and of the great genius who drinks himself to death over a one-woman love is more grotesque in itself than anything about Lautrec's real life.

But keeping movie cameras away from the "story of a genius" stereotype would be like keeping ants out of unprotected sugar in the country. The more-than-mythical assumption of the movies is that happiness is some vast, quasi-natural domain of sweetness which, by some machination of the devil or his equivalent, is repeatedly spoiled for human consumption. The artist becomes a natural apostle of this happiness no less than its natural enemy and victim; usually his agency (egotist that he is) is directed against himself. That the plastic imitation of life has something wicked as well as sublime, if not actually supernatural, about it, is an axiom of which vast numbers of people are convinced by their education and experience of the world. So it is with the spell cast by the sidewalk artist who sketches your head for a dollar, and so it is with the spell cast by Gauguin, who was so odd as to renounce modern comfort and a "respectable" existence to be poor and paint naked natives in the South Seas. The milieu which entranced Gauguin and unloosed his full genius, as imitated in Albert Lewin's Hollywood production of *The Moon and Sixpence,* has all the authenticity of a department-store display. Indeed, it is as bad as the use of the white-man-gone-native stereotype which Somerset Maugham vulgarly exploited for the novel on which the movie is based and which was submissively followed by Lewin.

Heaven forbid that serious movie-makers—so advanced and artistic that they insist on giving artists their due "dignity"—should be accused of deliberately catering to crude and vulgar myths about the artist! But what they do instead is cater to these myths, as it were, off the cuff and automatically. Such an advanced movie art as Lewin's, therefore, is an art of camouflage: sops more or less slyly handed to sophisticates in this day of enlightenment. Gone the nude model in the typical studio; gone the beret, the flowing tie, the loverlorn look that, if seen nowadays at the revivals, can make people laugh. People might easily laugh at Dietrich and the statue made of her in *The Blonde Venus* and at what happens to the work and its subject. But obviously the Pygmalion legend still appears in rented, albeit "correct," clothes. It is seen in *Rembrandt* when the artist persuades his housekeeper—dressed—to take Galatea's role.

What could be more correct as theatrical mummery, in *Rembrandt,* than Korda's careful pictorial reconstruction of Holland according to the Dutch painters?—the Dutch painters, that is, other than Rembrandt. Though the screen is quite capable of imitating Rembrandt's use of chiaroscuro (as was demonstrated in Dreyer's *Day of Wrath*) it was Vermeer and his lessers that Korda's photography sought to emulate. Certainly, according to the film laboratory's bible, Rembrandt looks better moving in a light to which photography is

50

thought best to correspond: dramatic contrasts, sharp silhouettes, "sculptural" clarity of form. And, indeed, he *is* seen better if by "better" is implied merely his outside. But this means, too, the "outside" of the familiar stereotypes in which the artist is the hero of a romance, not the hero of a life dedicated to creative work. Of course, Rembrandt (played by Laughton) is certainly shown as a painter, with a specific painter's presumed temperament, but it would be embarrassing to check the recorded facts of his life against the "facts" of the screen story about him.

In the movie process, the loss to truth by approximation, theoretically only a technical one, is willy-nilly a loss to truth in substance. It may seem only a technicality that Gauguin's eczema becomes, in movie and novel, Strickland's leprosy. But the solemnly silly insinuation is that leprosy is the physical allegory of an artist's spiritual corruption. Art as the image of corruption came ready-made to Lewin in Wilde's ambiguous fable, *The Picture of Dorian Gray*. But in this movie, the chief "authenticity" had nothing to do with Wilde's story. It was the employment of a legitimate painter, Ivan Albright, rather than some anonymous hack, to achieve the fatal Hallward portrait of Dorian down to its last stage of corruption. Granted that here we see a real painting (as we do not in the ridiculously faked Gauguins supposed to be Strickland-né-Gauguin's masterpiece going up in flames), it is still not the sort of corruption that Wilde visualized for his imaginary heartbreaker. Exactly the wrong aspect, the one of literal flesh, is emphasized. The truth was that Albright's talented obsession with decadent flesh was seized on by Lewin as a super-photogenic element. Striking in its own way, this was quite the wrong insight into Wilde's very artificial allegory of the corruption of love. Lewin was plausible to give Hallward, the fictional author of the portrait, a nice clean face and a velvet jacket, the latter typically Victorian, but the conversion of his pseudo-Sargent portrait (the first stage) into Albright's hyperbolic modern style was a false translation of what would be apt to happen, even magically, on a canvas in Wilde's era.

Romantic movie style hits the loneliness of an artist as "Oh, the loneliness!" and the pity of Lautrec's physique as "Oh, the pity!" and the Gauguinishness of Maugham's Strickland as "Oh, the Gauguinishness!" But, as it is hard to evaluate the self-isolating impulse of any specific artist or the way in which a man of genius is to be pitied, so it is hard to express the definition of any artist's identity. Gauguin did not always, or essentially, "loll" in the tropics when he wasn't painting: he published a newspaper protesting the colonials' treatment of the natives. It is hard even for serious prose biographers to do an artist both honor and justice.

A recent fashion, probably a result of Merezhkovski's *The Romance of Leonardo da Vinci*, has given rise to the use of a hybrid biographic fiction—doubtless also part of the current scientific mania to "verify" all aesthetic statements: a reactionary trend, I think, seriously damaging to the view of art. So much is actually "verifiable" in biographic items about the screen's new pretentious fictions about artists (including recent fictional biographies such as

51

The Titan, dealing with Michelangelo) that one is supposed to take the romantic element for granted; to let, so to speak, the romance "fall where it may." We are supposed to divine the romance of an actual man having magic in his hands and actually falling off the scaffold he used in the Sistine Chapel. The filmic attempts to interpolate "naturalizing" details, concocted in studio and laboratory, to provide a portrait of the artist while exhibiting his works has been, as such, uniformly disastrous, and may reach a stultifying vulgarity, as it did in brief art documentaries on Lautrec and Rodin, in which are represented the deserted glasses of Lautrec's liquor parties, whose contents he always mixed and drank off, and the hands of "lovers" (owners paid by the hour), supposedly the inspiration of Rodin's sculpture. The image of the artist thus transmitted is of a romantic fellow who *might* have worn a beret, been utterly handsome or monstrous, madly in love or morbidly self-isolated, whether he *did* or didn't, *was* or wasn't.

But if there is one thing to be had, of recent times, in screen representations of artists, it is variety. With the huge boom in color movies and the popularization of "modern" art, even esoteric art came unexpectedly into the spotlight, arrayed in Technicolor, in Hans Richter's fantasy, *Dreams that Money Can Buy.* This title was all too perfect an index that Hollywood's money-mindedness is not confined to Hollywood. In fact, its version of modern art as matrices of motifs borrowed from dreams came on the screen after Dali had been employed to illustrate a popular screen hero's dreams with his Surrealist-painting ideas. Richter had determined that modern art was as valid a relative of dreams as the movies and sought to demonstrate this relation in terms that admirers of Gregory Peck and Ingrid Bergman—if persuaded to look at them—could understand. As though to cement the authenticity of his interpretation, Max Ernst and Fernand Léger appeared in person in what amounted to prop-imitated versions of styles and imagery in their work. The question I ask is: Why should an artist's portrait be imaginatively authentic merely if he appear photographed with the objects whose genre corresponds to the objects and mode of behavior that inspire him? The notion seems to me pernicious. It is like having induced Michelangelo's ghost to materialize in order to get him to pose with some contemporary Italian gymnast.

The horrible cult of documentarism as "the truth" is firmly allied, alas, to the propaganda of the photograph as a parallel form of absolute persuasion. The authenticity of an artist's imaginative world appeared much more persuasively in Cocteau's *Blood of a Poet,* where the inner tensions of an artist's life were related to physical objects with something near the truth as verifiable through the artist's personal testimony. But Cocteau (Surrealist orthodoxy to the contrary notwithstanding) is a genuine if not always, of late, a perfectly sincere artist, and he, not another, made the film. A dazzling irony is secreted in his image of an artist who, while called a poet, is actually seen first as a painter, nude above the waist and wearing eighteenth-century breeches and white wig. Unquestionably, this costume came directly from Valentino as he appeared in a scene from the commercial film romance, *Monsieur Beaucaire* (the actor's face and hair, in addition, are much like Valentino's). Surely we have an interesting subtlety here: a film-maker who is an artist in his own right produces a convincing image of an artist by imitating the image of a screen star. Isn't Hollywood naïve to assume the opposite?—that by producing the image of a screen star it imitates a convincing image of an artist?

The intuition that an artist is someone with a "uniform," both mental and physical, is sound from a symbolic angle, but most dangerous in modern times. Just how dangerous can be gauged accurately from a social allegory disguised as a melodrama (or vice versa) which Carol Reed made in England, *Odd Man Out*. In this we see the Artist as a type next to an Ordinary Guy who commits offenses against political, economic and social laws. Robert Newton as the roughneck bohemian artist has been supplied with a costume-caricature out of Dickens: old clothes and long unkempt hair as bristling as his temperamental eccentricity. Dirt and drunkenness are once again the stamps bestowed on genius; dirt and drunkenness, that is, and wanton inhumanity. Perhaps the authors of this film fiction sat around congratulating themselves on their "realism" regarding "the" artist—isn't he as ruthless toward the human stuff he paints as a tyrant is, or was, toward a slave? An odd angle (one doesn't know whether anyone connected with *Odd Man Out* was aware of it) is that a valid literary legend does exist about the inhumanity of artists as a classic trait of theirs. Pierre Louÿs wrote a story about one of the late classic Greeks (Parrhasios, as I recall) who buys a slave just in order to torture him to death that he may copy his agonies for a painting of Prometheus bound. And he's very debonair about it, too. Possibly the painter's latent dionysianism in *Odd Man Out* is a reflection of this oblivious indulgence in cruelty. Anyway, he gets hold of the hapless fugitive of the title, now dying of his wounds, and strives to keep him in his studio so he can sketch his features for a painting of Christ on the cross. Whatever point of truth about the artist's nature may lie under this clownish allegory is quite dissolved by a glance over the artist's shoulder at some of his finished works, which are hideous.

A really wondrous point about those who are religiously conscientious about such "reality" on the screen is the laissez-faire they seem to have concerning the work exposed as the products of a presumed artist. The issue is that, if the artist involved is not a ranking talent, but any old dauber, then the type-characterization and the allegory in a film such as *Odd Man Out* are to be construed as a direct libel on artists and a more or less deliberate show of insolence. Of course, part of movie nonchalance about taking artists *un*seriously is due specifically to the exploitation of the popular unconscious hate for the artist as a being assuming certain superior, if not really antisocial, postures and prerogatives. The screen's *cachet* is torn between characterizing the artist as "just like you or me" or as a monster of mythical proportions, whether clown or disguised werewolf. Elements of both are also in *Scarlet Street,* where they are painted as much like the Old Adam as possible. Here is a sort of burlesque of the

53

Strickland prototype of a frustrated, neurotic, oh-so-vulnerable Sunday painter who is an undiscovered genius. Since the part is acted by Hollywood's leading art collector, Edward G. Robinson, this portrait of an artist has a special *brio* not altogether creditable to the parties involved. The tone of the film (made by a once reputable director, Fritz Lang) is that the fable of genius is basically an ambiguous fairy tale built on an impenetrable mystery—where does genius come from?—and that any comedy or melodrama to be made of it is quite legitimate because nothing about its values or meaning is certain.

The Sunday painter here is some kind of morally emasculate, convention-crushed barbarian who, though he has fallen hard for a pretty and pretty transparent hustler, believes in her and finally permits her to rob him of fame when (for money) she palms off his paintings as her own. This "genius" is thus discovered and celebrated on Fifty-seventh Street by proxy, and is perfectly happy until he finds out that his little lady has betrayed him with her boy friend, who had cooked up the plot in the first place. Then he murders her, escapes detection by a fluke, and begins the inevitable path to the gutter: no painter now and ruined by his conscience. The public, to be sure, is never so comfortable as when an artist ends up in a pit of corruption, whether it be Tahiti, a park bench or a lunatic asylum. What demon of sober judgment or unsober perversity, I wonder, induced Lang to cause to pass under our eyes again and again the most jejune and fakey daubs as the products of his hero's genius? They are fit images to place by the image of Robinson as the Sunday painter, whose Milquetoast personality here allows him only a brief moment in which to be the beast he constantly was in his gangster films.

The paintings are independent statistics that the story in which they appear is also a fraud. That Hollywood people can be blind to such glaring statistics while they cultivate their eyesight so assiduously for reading box-office receipts may seem to be in the nature of things, insofar as it is another example of that peculiar inconsistency which, indeed, may characterize genius itself, but which has back of it nothing of the animating, ordering and consolidating force of genius. What Hollywood cannot see (this defect permitting it to exhibit false and unconvincing images of the artist) is that the artist exercises a moral control over all contradictions and tragedies, personal and social, and that without such a control, he would not be empowered to create his masterpieces. The acceptance of the false-faces of art works that have to be clapped in as "props" of a romantic hero is simply one side of a coin, the other side being the rejection of the true artist for what he is: a powerful and deep human being whose "eccentricities" are the instruments he employs for his ascent and conquest of Parnassus.

It is a relief to be able to note, in a foreign movie, a representation of an artist whose only weakness appears to be a casual addiction to erotic commitments. It occurs in Colette's story, "Envy," in the distinguished Italo-French omnibus comedy, *The Seven Deadly Sins*, and tells in simple style how a painter discovers that the woman he has just chosen as a mate is ruled by the envy she feels for

54

his kind of life, both social and creative, because she is unfitted by character to share it. The episode makes a point of his business-like attitude toward his model, whom he draws in the nude, and that his wife has no thought or cause for sexual jealousy. Imagine, fans! Here is an artist—and rather bohemian, too, by the look of things—whose human ethic and whose libido shows no disagreement with the practice of his art; who, in fact, automatically relinquishes his true love because, beautiful and sexy though she is, she is allergic to artistic genius. Be sure: this is the heart, not the stuffed trouser legs, of being an artist.

THE
DREAM

more or less mythical

Dream Structure:
The Basis of Experimental Film

In the twenties, American amateur film-makers were inspired by the most serious examples of foreign film, notably *The Cabinet of Dr. Caligari* and Eisenstein's *Potemkin*. Considering the level of these main sources of inspiration, the result was not quite what might have been expected, and yet the reaction by those of aesthetic bent against the commercial motion picture had definite results in two inexpensive, noncommercial types of film: the cine-poem and the city-symphony. The former included trick stories told with objects, among them *Story of a Nobody* (Lewis Jacobs) and *No. 9413: The Story of a Hollywood Extra* (Florey-Vorkapich); simple essays in basic human drama, such as *Dawn to Dawn* (Stern-Byrne); or fantastic melodramas directly under the influence of Robert Wiene's *Caligari,* such as two tales from Poe and a psychological tour-de-force named *The Last Moment,* a lifetime rehearsed through the fleeting vision of a drowning man—an idea that might be, and probably has been, used in commerical film. What distinguishes the record of American Experimental film, which today has arrived at decided prestige and an accelerated growth, is the absence of the hokum and elaborate vulgarity that seemingly are indispensable to Hollywood; so, such an oddity as *The Last Moment,* however crude it might seem now, may be taken as free of the systematic effort to flatter the public by prettifying and simplifying; but above all, free of the aesthetic crime of translating the irrational element of human experience into cheap rational equivalents.

At the same time, through its superior honesty and direct feeling for pictorial beauty, Experimental film for the last four decades has been nothing if not artistically "proper" and even, in certain respects, "conservative." The complex visual patterns and vivid contrasts of the modern city inspired the early Experimentalists to seek artistic effects in pictures made by buildings, especially by means of extraordinary camera angles and arbitrary "framing," so that aesthetically their films approached a certain geometric style of abstract painting. At first, the city-symphony and the cine-poem existed side by side in a single domain of aestheticism. When films appeared such as Ralph Steiner's *H₂O,* entirely of water patterns, and Robert Flaherty's *Twenty-Four Dollar Island,* an impressionistic study of Manhattan, nature and man's world of machines and architecture seemed pleasant bedfellows. Abroad, abstract painting had come into its cinematic inheritance with films by painters: Fernand Léger's *Ballet Mécanique* and Marcel Duchamp's *Anemic Cinema,* a film made of painted spirals on revolving disks. But by the time the forties arrived, the city-symphony had definitely evolved into the informational and socially conscious documentary, usually one part moral reform and the other part newsreelism (the most interesting and competent example, *The City,* remains archetypal of this group). It is impossible to estimate how much "pioneering" film talent, aware of the pure values of the imagination, have been lost to commercial opportunities and their ingenuity wasted. Of course, some *has* been lost, and to their originators, those primitive efforts in the Experimental film must seem, now, like true enough excursions into Dreamland.

The far cries from the original artistic impulses of the American amateurs, so much impressed by the imagination of *Caligari* and the narrative art of *Potemkin,* became far, indeed. Despite weird dreams and other experiences of subjective and psychological nature, the approach by the Experimentalist to both art *and reality* has been more genuine than that of the commercial film-maker. Gradually, in view of thousands of productions down the years, Hollywood has managed to do at least *once* all the things that Experimentalists do consistently, intensively, and sincerely: *i.e.,* use of the vocabulary of "special effects" (dissolve, multiple exposure, distortion of image, stop-camera, and slow- and rapid-motion) as well as the basic film vocabulary, or "grammar," denoted chiefly by the term *montage.* Though technique is a lower-case Hollywood divinity, montage is still such a caviar quantity in the movie city that screen credits are given the experts who create it, just as the make-up man and the costumer are credited for their contributions. But technique in the montage sense used to be the bread-and-water of the cine-poem and the city-symphony, which as *labels* are more historic data than familiar usage.

These genres, truly, were nothing if not self-consciously formalist and even somewhat stiff and limited. All the same, reality—or a widely conceived "nature"—received the important tribute from the Experimentalists of not being distorted or sentimentalized—at least, so it was loosely assumed, and as loosely, and benevolently, we may regard them in present-day perspective. Yet actually a formidable road lay open to serious film-makers; it was, indeed, the road to Reality, but its patron deity was Science rather than Art, and its favorite muse Journalism. Thus came into being the school of documentary as distinct from that of Experimental: the worshipers of Fact as against the worshipers of Fiction, the latter becoming a dream to be shunned rather than explored. In observing so morally decisive a split, it is necessary to let perish the thought that Experimental film is to be adjudged "decadent," or merely "Surrealist,"

60

or (in any case) "obscure and incomprehensible," as it is still called by the backward.

The first nominally Experimental films to gain an international reputation, and to be shown in New York theaters as well as in educational institutions, were respectively Surrealist and quasi-Surrealist: Dali-Bunuel's *Andalusian Dog* and Cocteau's *Blood of a Poet*. Yet, having much "Surreality" in common, these films were built on opposed theories of aesthetic value; Cocteau never belonged to the official Surrealist movement in Paris. The use of the automatic image and the supernaturalist manipulation of bodies (active or inert, human or otherwise), as well as a general character of the poetic and fantastic, were traits these two films held commonly not only with each other but also with certain German and American Experimental films of the twenties and thirties; for example, with such an important work as *Lot in Sodom* (Watson-Webber) which applied a free poetic treatment to the Biblical legend. The evil reputation of decadence that has accrued so easily to artistic fantasy is the result of popular misunderstanding, based on the fear of inward self that sends distressed and frightened people to psychiatrists.

We must look to the canon of the dream itself to find what most draws and most repels people confronted with Experimental films. Of late years, in both foreign and native films, there have been numerous, more or less serious attempts to deal with dreams as clinical realities, but the clinical perspective is extraneous to artistic aims and the challenge to Experimental films must be met on its own ground. The orthodox criticism of so-called "Surrealist craziness" in these films is that, however ingenious or "pretty," this dominant element divorces itself from "reality." I would ask: Is a poem "real"? And answer: Yes, but it is seldom "realistic," even in narratives, for normally it uses many figures of speech, time-elisions (equivalent to a type of montage), and as a rule follows no rigid logical or temporal order. Modern poetry is especially complex and "irregular"; its basic order, like that of dreams, is the psychic order of association and suggestibleness. A "poem," one might remark, is what a cine-poem normally sets out to be.

With respect to emotions aroused by situations in drama or novel, and even by certain qualities within language itself, "poetic" is an adjective perhaps too easily applied. Even documentaries, we find, sometimes seem "poetic." One might speak of Robert Flaherty's last film, *Louisiana Story,* as poetic in certain of its sequences, and surely a recent work of documentary-fiction, *The Quiet One,* is threaded with a poetic human tenderness. But such adjectival qualifications do not define the chief purpose of either of these films, nor do they justify either by the distinctive standard of what may be called the Experimental cine-poem. A theme similar to Flaherty's in *Louisiana Story* appeared in the Hollywood film, *The Yearling;* while the latter was pretentious in certain ways, it was fundamentally, and in fact more consciously, what *Louisiana Story* was on its human side: the sex initiation of a pubescent boy—a vestige of ritualism as old as the hills.

61

As a thoroughly modernized, or quasi-scientific quantity, reality *is* much removed from the intensive aestheticism and fantasy world of Experimental film. Rightly speaking, however, reality includes imagination and mind, no less than their counterparts, fact and body. This comprehensive notion of reality might be termed an axiom utterly lost sight of by documentarists of puritanic temper when thinking of the technical ingenuity of Eisenstein's famous tale of the rebellious battleship Potemkin, and of the classic naturalistic outlines of Flaherty's pioneer records of exotic and primitive places; obviously, Flaherty's "primitive" reality has extended to current practice with results quite as unfortunate as fortunate. The most genuinely impressive facts about the work of these two men were that they took the filmic document as an adequate conception of life—not as the customary "short subject" but as a long subject, a "feature film"—and that they undertook the given task with a sense of rightness. The newly won prestige of the feature-length documentary was attached to the ill-fated Eisenstein work, *Que Viva Mexico!* unavoidably left to us only in fragments edited by other hands.

While a poetic reality emerges even through the warped forms of this Eisenstein project, it holds aloof from the cine-poem developed by practising Experimentalists through remaining securely in the everyday world of waking experience. The most persistent charge against the Experimental school is that, seeking fantasy and "night-mind" experience, they overexploit camera tricks on the formal side and hallucination on the side of content, and thus indirectly flout "reality." If reality be conceived at the level of the conventional, quasi-realistic novel, or of the facts read in the headlines, or of elaborate research in natural phenomena such as undertaken in recent years by the Disney studio, then—truly—Experimental film has very little to do, directly or indirectly, with reality. Obviously, on the other hand, reality should be taken at a higher level, from a deeper and broader viewpoint, than any visible in such models of expression as those just given, even though such models, like life itself, may supply facets on which the imagination can legitimately build.

The metaphor, the automatic image of the Surrealists, the phenomena of dreams or trance—this trio of elements make neither subjects for "scientific" inquiry nor yet "abnormal" fantasies for morbid exploitation by irresponsible persons. They signify cardinal points in the Experimental film creed. As true for every genuine artist, they are part of, or a technique for expressing, normal human experience, a working of the imagination projecting itself honestly in terms of a given medium. Reality is subjective as well as objective and, in an important sense, fiction as well as fact. In the determined, if not always fair, opposition of documentarists to Experimentalism, we find nothing but the rejection of the imagination as a significant form of experience in its own right. Among the greatest works of drama, poetry, and painting, nature and "normal" reality are indeed usually present but sometimes, notably, in symbolic forms of all kinds. The imagination uses facts only as starting points, as elements of composition, for a total form *expressing* if not always *identical with* a complete human experience.

As a human motive, art has its genesis within man, and without this basic innerness, man is not a living soul but a living thing. We see Maya Deren's typical heroine climbing over the roots of a huge tree lying near a beach, the latter—as she disappears above it—changing into a long table in a banquet room, on the top of which she crawls as through the underbrush of a forest. Afterward, we see her like a sleepwalker walking, running, climbing through a space periodically undergoing "magical" changes of scene; yet her action, the duration of the human kinesthesia, is continuous. This is a normal phenomenon in dreams and in poetry and in certain kinds of fiction, particularly in mythical poetry, where gods and magicians perform supernatural actions. The realistic power of the photographic image, on the other hand, is such that audiences are inclined to believe that reality is before them as in an ordinary mirror, passively recording ordinary images. Cocteau, however, has assured us that art's mirror is magical. "Magic" itself may be no longer, as once it was believed, visibly present in nature, but certainly many of our experiences, if we care to note or admit it, are uncanny and suggest in their spontaneous nature the structure of what is historically described as supernaturalism. It is a truism that the film camera is active as well as passive; that all we know as "film technique" is a product of cinematic inventiveness and manipulation formally parallel with the structural theory of actual magic. But cannot this widely known faculty of the camera to imitate magic, dreams, and hallucinations—cavalierly used by Hollywood as it pleases—be used to express reality primarily as *imaginative* reality, as poetry, and—in that visual style to which Experimental films give prominence—particularly as a sort of dance ritual, a ritualistic pantomime? The only element the dream finds necessary to reach order is *rhythm*. Art supplies this.

It seems only technically feasible, then, to let the camera photograph what it is, by its potential nature, fitted to reflect best. Camera trickery, so close to stage magic but much more, and infallibly, dextrous, is used often for comic effect in commercial films; the same tricks, indeed, appear copiously in French films *circa* 1900–1910, when the motion picture was only toddling. Yet the truth is that mental action itself may be of the so-called magical order. The barrier toward recognizing this is merely the superficial and limited, but hard, form the mind must adopt to move about for its daily tasks in the external world. One of the better Hollywood directors, John Huston, during an interview given some years ago to the *New York Herald-Tribune,* called attention to the fact that the movie camera imitates mental action in the way the gaze may automatically shift around the room. This was an understatement, obviously, for the camera is capable of imitating all mental impulses, whether as simple as a shifting gaze or as complex as a sudden hallucination. The well-known state of daydream illustrates a more or less voluntary surrender of the abstract visual attention to the meandering and sharp turns of the mind. Without necessarily noticing it, our minds are in the habit of "irrationally" mixing

63

thoughts and images of the external world, and entertaining disguised elements, which may or may not come to the surface, all day long.[1] When the Experimentalist deliberately utilizes this sort of mental behavior, he is lucky if he is not called, by most, odd, arty, or just futile.

To be sure, it must be granted that the Experimental genre is far from perfection even in some of its outstanding instances. It is often guilty of lapses of taste and oblique breakdowns in form; also, it seldom has ideas of much originality or great significance. Extenuation for these defects is present in the fact that material resources are usually very restricted among Experimental film workers and much too little financial reward is obtainable from the circulation of their products. It takes a great deal of courage and ingenuity to make the major effort typically required for a feature film; which is to say, to render a complete imaginative experience, in fifteen to twenty-five minutes' running time, at a cost of less than a thousand dollars, yet this is what talented American filmists such as Sidney Peterson, Willard Maas, James Broughton and Miss Deren among the older ones have done in recent years, and Curtis Harrington, Stan Brakhage, Kenneth Anger and Charles Boultenhouse among the younger ones. The quality of style and imagination in the bulk of work by these film artists cannot equal the classical Experimentals of Dali-Bunuel or Cocteau, nor such a unique imaginative effort as the late Jean Vigo's *Zéro de Conduite,* often revived in New York. If even Miss Deren's structurally strong and intensely personal films suffer from the Surrealist "cliché," it is only a variety of growing pains. In fact, perhaps the most encouraging factor of more recent American Experimentalism is the quality of dance ritual featured principally by Miss Deren's films.

The ritual instinct in man is inseparable from the rhythmic instinct; the human body naturally develops a choreography of gestures expressing its most intense, and especially its recurrent, emotions. The atmosphere of the private dream corresponds, in a certain obscure but exact sense, to the atmosphere of the public fantasy-work, such as romantic and modern ballets; Hollywood itself has become sensitive to this, Gene Kelly and others having exploited dance as a fantasy-impulse of dream-like character. Mankind, after all, has traditionally *danced* its greatest moments—at temple celebrations, at orgiastic fertility rites, in paying tribute to the dead. Dance is anciently an act of clairvoyance and magic. The choreographic inflection of ritual survives in church services as well as on the ballet stage; it appears significantly in the style of movement in a film already mentioned, *Lot in Sodom.* Human gesture suitable to poetic symbolism and nervous rhythms of emotion appears in James Broughton's satiric *Mother's Day* and Curtis Harrington's lyrically simple *Fragment of Seeking.* It is hard for the young and materially handicapped film worker to eliminate "amateur" notes in the bad sense. The attitude toward technique, more than the technical accomplishments themselves, ele-

[1] One wonders if, even in more enlightened circles, the lessons of Joyce's *Ulysses* have been properly learned.

vates the vision and forms the importance. *Mother's Day* makes significant use of objects as fetishes, and for the same spirit of using objects, both *Louisiana Story* and *The Quiet One* were to be applauded. Neither of the last two exploits dreams as such, being set in the usual, external, daily world, but they hold more than a few hints of the boy-hero's private world as a realm fertile in fantasy states.

In devotional rituals, man revives himself through his generations. The pernicious element in anti-Experimentalist reasoning is the same as that in Documentarist reasoning: dreams and hallucinations are split away from reality and, as the typical modern psychiatric film, *The Snake Pit,* misleadingly implied, are the natural resources only of psychopaths; of exiles from "normal, right-thinking" society. This, of course, is an old story in popular attitudes toward art, now given a characteristic timely twist by the prestige of the idea of psychic therapy. Nevertheless, poetic creators in all media have perennially "dreamt strange dreams" as did the Psyche of Greek legend, the subject of one of Gregory Markopoulos' films, and enriched vision with eternal ambiguity thereby. In dreams and spontaneous wild imaginings, man hunts down his innermost secrets, and by ritualizing this vein of the imagination, grows familiar with his inward, less conspicuous self. For its part, documentary film does almost nothing to mend the dream/reality split so insidiously and irresponsibly nurtured by Hollywood, while at least in theory, Experimental film is dedicated exactly to mending this split.

In Hitchcock's *Spellbound,* we found incorporated a Daliesque dream which indicated merely criminal guilt feeling and had to be treated strictly as a technical obstacle to the hero's happiness; psychoanalytically, it provided the clue to eventually proving his innocence of the crime involved. On the contrary, in the work of the Experimental film makers, the same sort of supernatural or magical condition as operated in this dream-sequence is used, without psychoanalysis, as the means *through which the protagonists are able to recognize their ultimate desires.* To know, as an audience, this supreme distinction, we must learn to interpret the symbols in Experimental films not as psychoanalytic, but as *poetic,* material. To assume them as having the same irrational premises that dreams begin by having, is itself a rational step toward making them contribute to cultural experience. This does not mean that their contents are to be treated as "latent" and "manifest," in the manner of psychoanalysis, and then translated into simple and concrete terms of logic; on the contrary, it means that, just as we take for granted the metaphors in a poem by Donne, Blake, or Hopkins, we are to accept the dream-structure element of the pictorial inventions of Experimentalism.

Film Form and Ritual as Reality

As we well know, the conditions of the commercial industry are conducive, through the feverish desire to provide what the public wants, to that extremism of pure device that borders on fantasy. Lately, focus has shifted from the DT's of the alcoholic to the swoon of the drug addict, but the emphasis remains largely statistical, external. Hallucination tends to be reserved for bold versions of Edgar Allan Poe heroes. And an "intellectual" farce like *What's New, Pussycat?*, huffing and puffing to outstrip the comic strip, treats psychiatry as if it were an invention of the Marx brothers. I refer here and now to more primitive film fantasies: the sort that, like *Down to Earth* with Rita Hayworth, shows the inventive minds of the studios innocently expanding in self-parody. Miss Hayworth is Terpsichore, enraged by a parody of herself in a Broadway musical and bent on vengeance. She lives in an appropriately organized Heaven, presided over by a monitor (a "Mr. Jordan") who is much like a specialty shop manager.

Serious modern dance was here opposed to the vulgar, jazzed up version of modernism. The representation of the Muses, including Terpsichore, was of course not itself serious but done with the tongue-in-cheek supernaturalism that characterized such more significant comedies as England's *The Man Who Could Work Miracles* and René Clair's American-made *It Happened Tomorrow*. As for *Down to Earth*, it should be noted that, like more than a few other Hollywood exhibits, it was unconsciously gauged to be parable-fantasy of what happens to the conceptions of serious art within the confines of the movie studios. Thus, Terpischore's "real goods" is itself a Hollywood version of serious ballet, so that the revue-ized version of Terpischore's ballet, seen in the same film, is but one farther remove toward vulgarity.

The British production, *Stairway to Heaven*, was set in an elaborate vein typical of film fantasy. The movies hesitate to accept a perfectly serious bona-fide supernaturalism, but do not feel inclined to neglect a genre so obviously suited to the nature of the medium. After all, what is so mechanically close to the principle of ancient animism and that of latterday stage magic, alike, as

66

the film device of double exposure and such effects as the materialization of a vapor into a person (as we saw in Clair's *I Married a Witch*)? *Stairway to Heaven* made use of the stop-camera device very ingeniously to indicate a supernatural order of time, but it portrayed heaven as though it had been predicted that way by H. G. Wells.

The purely aesthetic value of movie supernaturalism is not in question. At the same time, we cannot, if we take the position of serious analysis, fail to note that many film devices (see Sergei Eisenstein's book *The Film Sense*) have a basic kinship with literary and plastic devices in painting and poetry, notably with metaphor itself. Hence, in the light of tentative belief in the world of the supernatural, film supernaturalism must rely on the brand of pathos-comedy. It behaves as though to say: "All this may be mere hallucination, equivalent to myths and dreams, but wouldn't it be marvelous if it were really so? Meanwhile we may sympathize with the dilemmas of those who manage to find themselves with supernaturalist experiences—thus, logically, with super-naturalist beliefs." Unquestionably, official religion must oppose the light-mindedly ambiguous view of spiritual and divine being that we habitually find in the movies—but such a criticism is not the present objective.

An English studio has produced a film which, making use of the above-mentioned pathos-comedy technique in melodramatic fashion, gives an *archetypal* form to the supernatural patterning of commercial movies. It is *Dead of Night,* so very significant because it not only has a typical kind of supernatural-ism, but also reveals in terms of parable the film mechanisms which unite film with the mechanism of dream and of supernatural hypothesis.

Both dream literature and psychology, especially psychoanalysis, have made us familiar with *the recurrent dream.* This is the basic subject as well as the over-all plot pattern of *Dead of Night.* The film opens with the shot of an automobile approaching us along a country road; it stops; the driver, its single occupant, looks at a large residence set back from the road; he turns the car into the driveway. . . . It develops, after he becomes a member of the tea party going on inside the house, that he is an architect who has been invited for a week end to discuss additions to the owner's house. But it also develops that this architect is experiencing in self-evident reality a dream which he has repeatedly had—a dream ending in death and terror.

To grasp the form at once, it will do to say that everything happens as fore-told by his dream, even to the point of his killing someone and violently striking a young girl; the latter incident takes place in his own hallucination following the murder and constitutes the chaotic terror of a climax typical of dreams. Indeed, as the gentleman in question suddenly wakes up at home in bed, it is evident that what we have seen has all been a dream . . . *but* . . . the tele-phone at his bedside rings, and we observe that he receives that original invi-tation which supposedly had actually drawn him out to the country and to the house of his recurrent dream.

We do not have a startling novelty here, certainly. But the device has an automatically attractive ingenuity. Spectators of this movie, I had occasion to note, were inclined to exclaim "Ah!" and marvel as people do when they hear a bona-fide supernatural tale, momentarily entertaining the hypothesis that somehow the reality-principle may be involved. Indeed, the story has involuted reality and dream in such a way that the basic condition of supernaturalism as distinct from "naturalism," or the verifiable phenomena of life, is quite lost sight of. There has been a brilliant tour de force of the kind to make us associate it with sleight-of-hand on the stage; it is in a sense a perfectly *manifest* phenomenon, and so ingenious is it that comparing it with the thing we customarily know as "truth" or the content of "belief" seems redundant. Yet, of course, we have reflective wit, which enables us to descry the nature of the trick and criticize it.

Viewing *Dead of Night* from one standpoint, we can easily condemn it as sheerest melodrama which goes out of its way to mock the commonest truths of life; hence, it is morally frivolous. Perhaps only that strange sect, the Theosophists, could be persuaded to take a systematic and wholly approving moral view if challenged to do so. There is, otherwise, the classic objection that in any case such phenomena are so rare as to be insignificant to man as a society. If an average member of the movie audience were asked pointblank if he "believed" that such phenomena as in *Dead of Night* could be real, he would be bewildered and probably answer that he was unable to decide. But he might go on to say that the separate episodes preceding the murder-and-hallucination sequence of the architect, and told by other guests of their own experiences, held phenomena which *might* be true; just so does one run across people who tell stories of supernatural things, usually involving telepathy, to whose authenticity they can swear first-hand.

Now let us examine the plot mechanism in the round. The fact is that it is precisely by the anticlimactic device of the architect's awaking to reality, as though the whole film had been a dream, *only to have reality reproduce the mechanism of the dream,* that we are allowed to accept the whole thing as something more than a tour de force or form of fantasy. Because if the architect had conclusively awakened to reality, the original plot-hypothesis of his "dream come true" would have thereby been *part of the dream,* and so the film would have taken a purely cynical view of supernaturalism, since by the same token, the supernatural stories told by people met at the house party would have been ingredients of this dream. The architect would merely have dreamt about having a dream—not such a rare phenomenon. It is only through the phone's ringing at the architect's bedside and the actual occurrence of the invitation, that we are once more, supposedly, in the "real" world of dream-come-true.

The flavor of this movie strongly suggests the work of the playwright, Luigi Pirandello, except that the latter juggles with the involution of fiction and reality exclusively in *subjective* terms of the psychic convention. As I say, the net effect of *Dead of Night* is that of playing with a serious hypothesis as though it were a trick. One may recall Thomas Mann's *Mario and the Magician* as a work which attached serious symbolic significance to the antics of a stage hypnotist. The figure of Mann's mountebank had a sinister quality which portrayed the artist type he was supposed to represent as one who "plays" with things that in the real-life dimension are deadly earnest. In fact, the magic in *Dead of Night* replaces hypnotism with ventriloquism. However, the great disparity between Mann's purpose and that of the makers of *Dead of Night* is that the latter's ostensible subject matter is not the normal life of society but certain exotic phenomena on the margin, the doubtful realm that scientists claim (and artists are ready to agree) exists only in man's imagination. The tragic irony in both Mann's story and the plays of Pirandello is that men are victims of their illusions and sometimes really die because they cannot correctly identify reality. A law of reality is seen to triumph—even if it be the absolute insanity that overtakes Pirandello's "Henry IV." As Henry IV also, our architect is driven to kill.

In the case of the movie under discussion, while reality is a necessary hypothesis (that is, the world we know is the inevitable setting even of such events as shown), the *intellectual* nature of reality is left in doubt. Man's decision as to the character of reality is shown psychologically at the moment when he is unable to tell dream from reality, yet there are no consequences of this "moment," either moral or philosophical. *Life merely goes on.* The cyclic feeling of the film becomes *absolute* when we see the opening shot repeated at the end: the auto approaches us along the road and stops as the architect looks toward the house. The only implicit reality is the eternal recurrence of—this is important— a *harmless* dilemma. The architect, *ergo,* may not know dream from reality in the terms of this fiction, but at least he is guaranteed eternal recurrence—a whole lifetime of waking up, first to experience great relief, and then to realize that he is to undergo the "nightmare" events of the dream, at the end of which nevertheless he is assured (as though to be rescued from eternal damnation) exemption by reawakening. No judgment of the nature of reality, no formulation of the reality-principle, has been made except to leave self-manifest that life has two *qualities:* "reality" and "dream"; the relationship between these qualities is in absolute suspense.

Now, considering that a psychiatrist is one of the characters in the movie and that it is he who upholds the skeptical views of science in face of the general inclination of those present to credit supernatural phenomena, it is only fair to take a more advantageous view of the proceedings than was available to this unfortunate psychiatrist, who chanced to be the victim selected for the architect's murder. In the view of psychopathology, the original mechanism of the architect's representation that reality was carrying out the events of his recurrent murder dream *might itself be a fiction:* a common enough paranoid phenomenon. Resistance to criminal deeds may become so desperate in certain psychotic types that eventually they are prepared to say that they have

69

"dreamed" what they finally decide to do. In this light, it may be remarked that the anecdotes in support of the supernatural hypothesis by other members of the house party are themselves explicable on a level more profound than any suggested by the psychiatrist.

Not to go into too many plot details: the experience of one man is classified by the psychiatrist himself as a trauma of the death fear, appropriately enough having befallen an automobile racer who has almost died in an accident. A lady tells of an experience dealing with the hallucination of a man who is first her fiancé, then her husband; a psychoneurotic delusion transparently based on an impotence neurosis, which first makes him fear marriage and then become irrationally jealous of his wife. The third anecdote is told by the psychiatrist, its supernatural hypothesis being explained, accordingly, scientifically. This story happens to be the only one of complete authenticity in the film, and while most unusual, its individual components are quite within the realm of possibility.

Its basis is the homosexual complex of a ventriloquist, whose dummy becomes the object on which he projects his guilt. When another ventriloquist in good-natured sport uses the dummy for *his* voice-trick, the first ventriloquist becomes fixated on this man, whom he now identifies with his guilty desires. As a result, his struggle with his guilt takes the form of imagining the dummy, called "Hugo," has an independent existence and wishes to become partner to the other ventriloquist. The "rival" ventriloquist receives proposals made in Hugo's voice, apparently on Hugo's lips, proposals of which the dummy's owner shows signs of being intensely jealous. Here too is a familiar enough mechanism. It is quite logical that, eventually, his career ruined and still fixated on the other ventriloquist, the guilt-ridden man should try to murder his rival under the delusion that he has "alienated" the dummy's affections. This, indeed, is what happens. Finally, the dummy being restored to his owner in jail, the ventriloquist destroys him after Hugo tells him he has definitely decided to leave him for his rival, who is recuperating from his bullet wound. In a truly appalling dénouement, the ventriloquist, having fallen into catalepsy, is aroused only to greet the other ventriloquist, who visits him, in the voice and with the facial expressions of Hugo. . . . The transference is complete, the guilty desire now in the open.

The presence of this brilliant episode in the plot serves to root the movie indisputably in a domain opposing common pathology to the supernatural convention; surely, nothing so eloquent or artistic as this episode has been made about a pathological human being in film. Its force is bound to affect our view of the other, less convincingly real, episodes. The supernatural element in the ventriloquist's story is analogously weaker than that in either of the other two stories; it is only that the dummy apparently goes to the rival ventriloquist's room on his own locomotion. The psychiatrist plausibly suggests that without being precisely aware of it, Hugo's owner took him there himself so as to be able to make his accusation and stage his drama.

70

What I wish to point out about these independent minor plots is the significance of their *form* rather than of their *substance*. We can analytically identify their substance, as I say, with pathological mental phenomena. The peculiarity of their form in this movie, internally connected with the over-all plot (itself explicable on psychoanalytic grounds), is *that the supernatural element can in all cases be interpreted in terms of film itself, that is, in terms of its technical forms, its quality of illusion.*

In the episode of the automobile racer, the subject of the hallucination obtains it while lying alone in his hospital room, reading a book; he looks at the clock ticking by the bed and observes that apparently eighteen hours have passed after only a few minutes' ticking. Something makes him rise and go to the window, whose curtains his nurse has drawn before leaving him. He throws them back and looks out upon the afternoon light of a quarter to four rather than the dark of about ten at night. Looking down into the street, he sees a hearse . . . and so on. Now this hallucination has occurred in a window space that has exactly the shape (and even the opening curtains) of a movie screen. We may note further that it is precisely in a movie that we see day follow night after a matter of seconds. It is likewise at the movies that we see artistic material often fantastic and hallucinative in character; it would, moreover, be amazing to witness later, as the racing driver did in this case, the virtual repetition of the vision in actual experience.

In the next episode, the frame of the hallucination, being a large mirror, has the approximate proportions, if not also the straight sides and right angles, of a movie screen. And we recall that film itself *is* a mirror. The Chippendale style of the mirror in the story merely conforms with the character of the hallucination, which is a room of the last century. Whenever the man who is first fiancé then husband looks into this wedding gift from his wife, he sees not his own room in which he stands, but a somber Victorian affair which we learn later is presumably that of a gentleman who once owned the mirror and the room seen therein, and whose delusions of his wife's infidelity caused him to murder her. It is entirely appropriate that the previous drama of sexual jealousy and attack, which the young husband proceeds to repeat in his own life, should be of a kind, and with a setting, typical of horror melodramas seen of late years in British and American movies; *Gaslight,* for example, is memorable. This plot and its features make a perfect parable for the effect of such melodramas on psychotically inclined individuals who go to see movies. I am not suggesting the general plausibility of such a parable of actuality but merely indicating the logic of its form in this place, so significant (as I shall show) in the over-all pattern of this movie.

The relevance of the ventriloquist episode to the film medium is fairly obscure, yet certainly not without validity. It is not merely that a symbol of *the actor,* the dummy, is present; this would also be true of the legitimate theatre. It is that one of the faculties of film is the widely known "dubbing in" of voices,

71

usually done when a star actress, having no singing voice of her own, must let another's voice appear on the sound-track if she is required to sing, and now frequently true of foreign movies, which are "dubbed" in the language of the country of import. This is a parallel of ventriloquism. Moreover, we must identify here, as in the other episodes, the constant factor of *projection* (common to the mechanism of mind and film) of which *the window* and *the mirror* provide the film-like scene in the first and second episodes; in the third, the symbolic figure of the dummy is the "scene" of the projection—that he is an actor, and that his voice is dubbed in according to the ventriloquistic mechanism, are facts merely enhancing the aptness of his use. Is it not possible for neurotic homosexuals to project their repressed or unconscious desires arbitrarily onto others, especially on an actor or actress seen in the movies?—and in secret fantasy, perhaps, to interpret a masculine business partnership in a movie as something perverse? We cannot fail to recognize the frequency of such phenomena in our society.

I am not trying through this analysis to impute to *Dead of Night* either ulterior motives, on the part of its makers, or practical consequences; nor am I offering, strictly speaking, either a sociological or "clinical" analysis. Such factors are logically corollary to my main purpose, which is to indicate the striking degree of unconscious symbolism in this film as a parable of the experience of movie spectators who face a screen *on which fictions are projected*.

The fourth sequence is the deliberate yet unmotivated murder of the psychiatrist by the architect who is the "author" of the dream. After all, we must note that the episodes related by the others have apparently had no place in the dream proper; only their images have been present as members of the house party; the architect does not mention their own stories as having been part of his dream. The climax for the architect is to be left alone with the burly psychiatrist (as, ostensibly to be "psyched," he is so left) and to strangle him, after which he experiences his own hallucination: an imaginary young-people's party in which he plays the one who hides in a game, then tries to violate the girl who discovers him; this sequence is significantly given the mad air of a dream through typical film devices of crazy angles and sharp foreshortening. When the architect is mobbed for his attack, he wakes up in a sweat of terror (as I mentioned) at home in bed. It is needless to tabulate this man's psychotic symptoms, which indeed might have led in reality to the murder and the attendant hallucination.

But several things are evident in relation to movie conventions and ritual. With kaleidoscopic rapidity, before his own hallucination ends, the architect fantastically identifies himself with each episode he has heard related by the other guests. Hence I propose the architect as the arch-symbol of the movie-goer in *Dead of Night*—not necessarily as the paranoiac which the internal elements of the case make him out, but rather as an innocent movie-goer, a "normal citizen" whose neurotic proclivities fleetingly induce him, via the aesthetic convention, to connect himself with the monstrous fantasies he is accustomed to see on the screen.

We are familiar in the movies with the alternately innocent-looking and straightforwardly weird-looking edifice which turns out to be a nest of horrors, and which at the beginning some intrinsically innocent wayfarer stumbles upon, perhaps in a storm. If we take this architect as the archetypal movie-goer, and we imagine him entering a movie house rather than a manor house, we would find it just as plausible if he then asserts, as he *does* in *Dead of Night,* that he recognizes the people, the house, etc., for the simple reason that he recognizes them *generically,* as obvious elements of "another of those horror mystery stories." His "certainty" that various things will happen is again a certainty about approximate things, a result of his familiarity with the rigid plot-patterns of this type of movie. The orthodox theory of recognition admits, indeed, the common factor of substitution of particular identification for general identification (a factor, incidentally, which the psychiatrist brings up in reference to the racing driver's story).

Let us suppose, furthermore, since it seems strongly indicated, that our movie-goer has a private, if not deadly, neurosis of his own, and hence that he may more willingly lend himself to the elements of one screen fantasy than to the elements of another. I need hardly point out in passing that, of all forms of popular artistic entertainment, that of television and the movies is most akin to the conditions of private daydream, so it would be definitely apt that our "hero" is an architect, one who wished to modify the "public edifice" of dream with his own private "additions." Especially since psychiatric films have won popularity, and since a psychiatrist is an undeniable figment of social reality linking dream fantasy with hidden truth, our architect movie-goer may, in a spirit perhaps of resistance to having his private life "scientifically" investigated, imagine the psychiatrist he finds in some film as his personal antagonist, and may identify himself as his screen murderer; if said psychiatrist isn't actually murdered, perhaps the movie-goer believes the murderer *should have* made him his choice.

Such a mental pattern for our movie-goer is necessarily a mere hypothesis as *he* is a hypothesis for the architect. Yet the present procedure of analogy serves this function: the involuted dream/reality (or fiction/reality), so ambiguously presented in *Dead of Night,* becomes coherent, *a part of verifiable reality,* if we regard the whole movie as a parable of this kind; namely, a parable for the practical workings of an aesthetic convention. It is easy to imagine that Mr. Average Citizen, faithful movie-goer, can—with the fantasy projection of Walter Mitty, the hero of Danny Kaye's movie—overcome a psychiatrist, if necessary, by strangling him; especially, we may note, if he inclines sentimentally to a frivolous but lingering belief in the supernatural. Here we have the conflict between the psychiatrist and the others within the film reflected in the mind of a spectator "pulled both ways." One might even agree that, on a cold-blooded

73

level, the movie-goer resents the "technical" introduction of a scientific agent, the psychiatrist, whose role is to explain away or cure all the fabulous phenomena (and perhaps prevent the implicit rapes) which the movie-goer's imagination enjoys and to the "belief" in which his mind secretly clings. It is not only that Frankenstein's monster is a scientific dream realized but that, according to another aspect of the fiction, he is a libidinal dream realized.

The movie-goer returns home as the architect awakes—to realize that it is all, perforce, a dream, a fiction; something both horrible and attractive, yet somehow inevitable. Surely enough, the phone rings. No matter how banal the movie last seen, the current one may be better—and there is always the sneaking hope that "something real" inheres in all the fantasy, that the natural conceals the supernatural as cleverly and as easily as a magician's cloak a squawking goose. In a way, no doubt, it does. So he heeds the automatic "invitation," he gets in his car, he arrives. . . . In the theater, he sees the old, familiar faces flash on the screen.

The importance of *the continuous performance* in film houses should not be underestimated. In *Dead of Night* it has been ingeniously associated with an *eternal* idea of recurrence: the beginning again of the cycle which we see as the architect stops his car, gazes at the familiar house, and the action fades out at the point it faded in. The principle of the old-fashioned serial, with its constant renewal of effort and typical situations, was identifiable with that of life itself—especially with the go-getting psychology of American life. Of course, so far as any religious conception of recurrence goes, *Dead of Night*, even with its factor of supernaturalism, is a parody. But *that* is its point in this analysis.

The movie-goer I have proposed as substitute for the architect is also a *parody* of him, as any spectator must be a parody of any character in whose role he may incongruously imagine himself. Is not Hugo, indeed, a parody of his master's hidden personality? In the same way, the character of Walter Mitty in Danny Kaye's film is a parody of the true-adventure heroes whom he worships and emulates in his daydreams. Mitty is a man whose imagination has been hypnotized not by reality but by the movie version of it. The complex irony is that he is a parody within a parody, as the architect's dream is a dream within a dream. For, in effect, the comical Danny Kaye in the role of Mitty is a parody of other movie heroes who, in turn, are parodies of the aviators and surgeons they impersonate in more or less serious screen stories. Just so, Rita Hayworth as Terpsichore is a parody of serious ballet dancers, as, in turn, the musical-comedy dance in her film is a parody of Miss Hayworth's "Terpsichorean" choreography. This parody-principle is as involuted as the reality-principle of the thesis of *Dead of Night*. The movies are not only a hotbed of reality-parody but of *self-parody*. I have tried to show that this film's reality-principle is genuine—and ascertainable by the same standards as we determine parodies—if we assume the premise of the reality of a *form:* the filmic form and its psychic spectator-components.

74

The Lady Called "A"; Or If Jules and Jim Had Only Lived at Marienbad

Last Year at Marienbad is not the most artistic film I know but it is the most self-consciously artistic film I know. According to its author's own published declaration, it was written literally as a film script; there was perfect harmony between the director, Alain Resnais, and the author, Alain Robbe-Grillet, who pronounced the resultant product as virtually perfect. The relationship between the two men is obviously to be compared to that between the designer of an objet-d'art on paper and its execution by someone else in the materials designated. *Marienbad* as a book is a proud, perhaps too proud, piece of prose, pretending like the king in the fairy tale that he is not naked but clothed respectably in gorgeous attire. The truth is, the illustrated script—contrary to the logical superstition of Robbe-Grillet that only seeing and hearing, not reading, is really believing *Marienbad*—offers a most inoffensive and adequate substitute for the actual movie. To me, it is the same purse-proud piece of couture—like a Dior (excuse me, a Chanel) gown made at home by two clever spinsters. Robbe-Grillet's script, with over 140 illustrations, is simply an Ohrbach's ad for what you can buy at the theatre and wear home. On the other hand, it is also possible, in the theatre, to feel like a voyeur at a fashion show. One of Robbe-Grillet's books (and not, I think, by chance) is called *The Voyeur*.

What do real fashion editors, and other aesthetic critics, feel at a fashion show? Don't they imagine somewhere in their heads that each mannequin is heroine of a hypothetic romance—with, preferably, a sumptuous, dazzlingly dated background speaking of another time's glamors? The destiny of each gown—as the high fashion magazines have developed a thousand ways of telling its readers—is, naturally, to grace an actual woman, who uses it to seduce all kinds of admirers; so with each new hairdo, lipstick, and skin-cream as parts of a personal ensemble to fit into some gilded, "baroque" and faraway, but nominally very real mirror, ballroom, salon, and bedroom. The ultimate is also to be able to watch a classic play (it might be, says

75

Robbe-Grillet, something by Marivaux!) and that is what everybody, when the Marienbad film opens, is doing: watching a deluxe play in deluxe et cetera.

For sublime unconsciously promoted chic, well-behaved, and tastefully well-behaved to the point of painfulness and boredom, the Robbe-Grillet-Resnais film is the perfect item for—not for *Vogue* readers themselves, not for the world as seen and seeing in *Harper's Bazaar,* but for the world enclosing those readers and sightseers, the world consciously and unconsciously collaborating with it. Technically, there is no room for *New Yorker* magazine jokes in *Marienbad,* nor for *New Yorker* gayety or cynicism, which tends to slice the world into hunks suitable for a casseroled society. The actions of the film, "rape" scene, "murder" scene, and all, are nicer, more restrained even, than Command Performances these days. Suppose the Marienbad lady (who the script is obliged to call "A") does get plumped over the side of the bed heels up: the camera reacts like a gentleman; that is, it quickly looks away, as imperturbably kind and considerate as the lady's guardian, the gentleman who always wins the game against the man who wishes (again?) to seduce her.

But why beat about the bush just to see the petals fly? This film is a movie masquerading as the gimmick known as "Haven't we met somewhere before?" As this sort of gimmick (honest as a naked fairy tale) it is the most refined instance one could imagine. Even when, at last, its reluctant victim, the lady, seems persuaded to believe, and thus repeat, it, everything is so formal and ordinary that it might be stereo-scented without offence to the least credulous. A lady behind me at the theatre was, now that I think of it, stereo-scented. As for screams, what's a scream in the night at this juncture of planetary hostilities? Purely operatic, of course. And the silence around it! That's the way *any* well-bred company would behave. The quality is as irreproachable, and archaic, as that of a butler who has been through a couple of family generations—and doesn't gossip in the kitchen, either. The waiters at Marienbad are just as impeccable. The one who picks up the pieces of the glass broken by *A* conforms with the professional suavity one sees on every inch of the wide screen. The reality of *Last Year at Marienbad* is that one never needs to be reminded that this is a film. It reeks of being a film. It could not possibly get away with pretending to be anything else. It's honest in the way that a dress is a dress, a woman a woman, sex sex, Chanel Chanel, and life a dream—haven't innumerable movies said so?

But if a dress is a dress, the logical-minded may inquire, why is life a dream (not, that is, a documentary film)? Because now you see it, now you don't. This is incontestably the psychological law by which the *Marienbad* film is made. That being so, why should not love—good, bed-ridden love—begin and end with a series of unconsummated embraces, which "only the cinema could really *show*, etc. etc." The one surefire device (that made even Bosley Crowther glow before *Marienbad*) is that it's simple-minded as a set of opposite mirrors, *morally* simple-minded enough to accept them, more-over, as an ultimate aesthetic law. What is seen in them, however, might con-ceivably make a difference. Let us look, then, at the subject of this amusing and highly workable toy. I should say the subject is the hysterical fear of action which paralyzes people into the minimum of significant moves. If the lady screams at a fantasized broken balustrade and a lover shattered on the ground, one might call *that* a significant move. But is it? The script says, "Now the scandal is enormous." Obviously the author exaggerates. He can afford to do so because everybody, including most of the audience, is con-spiring with him to minimize exactly the scandal's "enormousness." The silence was so dense that not even the background noises would have muffled an openly said "Pooh!" Not to those sitting nearby anyway; I am sorry I didn't think of saying it.

A's scream is very significant. I interpret its significance as a wish-fulfil-ment to be rid of that harassing thing (unbecoming to one who is supposed to have everything) that is action, choice, the catharsis of a passion. Robbe-Grillet makes a great mistake by referring to his characters' "passion." If Post Office were the fatal game played in *Marienbad*, it would be just as suitable a vehicle for the passions of the love triangle as the game that is played. Passion is not for those who have everything but for those who want something else and are passionately unafraid of exhibiting the fact. The moral code disciplining all the desires in *Marienbad* is: Don't seem not to have everything. Delphine Seyrig's very lipstick seems to scream her deter-mination to obey this principle. Doesn't she *know* she has everything, even an enviable hairdo? So why, in God's name, should this man be telling her that a "repeat performance" is necessary? If they did have each other, last year at Marienbad, they've had each other and therefore they have every-thing. Insolent! If she didn't leave her Sweet Life with her "guardian" then, why leave it now? You cad, you would try to take advantage of a woman by feeling her breasts! Isn't it an old act and isn't it a bit corny? A Chanel was always a Chanel, is a Chanel, and always will be a Chanel, at least until it falls apart. Did Orson Welles or Eric von Stroheim ever repeat themselves? No. Mostly because people wouldn't let them. Once is enough, and if not enough, too much. Besides, what about *next* year? It would be just like you to come back and want it again.

I trust I've gotten my point across without being as assiduous, or as banal, as Resnais' film. My tale, at least, does not run an hour and thirty-three minutes. François Truffaut's *Jules and Jim* runs even longer than that, and so does Jacques Rivette's *Paris Is Ours*. Rivette does not have the economic sensibility of true couture. Yet his and Truffaut's films, just mentioned, are simply homely, less elegant, deliberately rude variations on the same theme as that harmonized at Marienbad. Jules' and Jim's Paris is the Bohe-mians' Marienbad. I think it by no means certain, taking Marienbad as my filmic authority, that Catherine actually drives herself and Jim off that broken bridge to finish the action. The evidence of the cremation of their bodies, and Jules' lone funeral cortège, is inadmissable as conclusive. Might it not just as well be Jules' fantasy—or Catherine's—if life *is* a dream? The Resnais film and the Truffaut film are not without striking resemblances. There seems something as eternal about Jules and Jim as about high fashion, which Jeanne Moreau illustrates as chic middle class circa World War I. Part of the amusement of *Jules and Jim* is Moreau's get-ups, which have personality and look downright bizarre—quite in the spirit of *Harper's Bizarre* nowadays. Again and again, she seems a subject taken not by Truffaut's cameraman but by a fashion mag photographer.

All the broad, naïve sweetness of *Jules and Jim* (which at least seems to have been Truffaut's object) disappears if we consider the meat of the matter in *Paris Is Ours*, the Jacques Rivette film mentioned above. And what is said "meat"? It's the basic if obliquely stated truth of things, and this is: When books are burned (for example, the Nazi book-burning that is a movie-within-a-movie in *Jules and Jim*), when film studios are burned (as, so to speak, 20th Century Fox has been), when seeming drastic demolitions of other kinds are accomplished (like Catherine's fatal plunge), there tends to be nothing with which to replace them. Is there more than one Elizabeth Taylor? No. Is there more than one Marilyn Monroe? No. Did the Nazis have books really replacing those they burned? No. Can you blame the lady for wanting to stay at Marienbad, no matter what happened there last year?

The present—that is, *this* year—is unable to revive the past with any feeling of success or good conscience, a fact which is so significant because little seems alive *except* the past. Take the paranoid hysteriacs and contaminated companions herded together in *Paris Is Ours*, which would be a better title with a question mark after it. These repressed psycho-neurotics have nothing, it would appear, but *memories* of having been an underground resistance, spies, Spanish Loyalists, Communists—what have you. The audience never gets a hint of what they have been or are, or *think* they have been or are, beyond a faint insinuation that some of the unhappy victims might be exiled enemies of the Franco regime. Two men in the film apparently commit suicide under circumstances giving their circle of acquaintance the suspicion that the cause might have been sheer depression or perhaps political persecution. A relative or a friend, on the other hand, tends to believe that they were murdered by secret agents of some kind. Yet the film makes clear another possibility still: they might have killed themselves from *delusions* of persecution. In fact, the third death is revealed definitely as a murder. One of the principals is in flight from a real or imaginary danger (anyway, one he has always feared) and another of the principals, a woman, is helping him escape. What is supposed to happen—though it is as illusively presented as any moment in *Marienbad*—is that the woman stops her car at an isolated spot in the country and shoots her companion dead. If Rivette hadn't already been lavish in suggesting otherwise, one might think that it were the climax of an international-spy thriller, in which true identities are at last revealed, and the agent for one nation gets the drop on the other: *bang!*

The silence surrounding *this* climactic incident is more than polite: it's creepy. And Rivette means it to be. There's no smile to wipe off your face as when you see the very last of Catherine and Jim. Unless I am much, much mistaken you'll feel, as *Paris Is Ours* flicks off, as though your face couldn't get any blanker. Maybe you'll be sorry for the poor little sister of the man just murdered; she's quite bewildered by all the shenanigans, and when told by the murderer that she doesn't know why she (the murderer) did it, the poor thing looks quite forlorn. Yet a remarkable quality exists in *Paris Is Ours*. This is the neutrality of the feelings evoked by it, and seemingly even involved in it. There are no "good guys," really, but one, and he is engaged only (apparently) in producing Shakespeare in French. Maybe this is sinister enough in the eyes of his enemies (if any); at any rate, socially, he belongs to the "artist class." However, with one thing and another, including a slippery cast, his production plans are wrecked. Does he then commit suicide in what one must take as "aesthetic" despair, and is this engineered by political enemies, as the film hints is possible, or just by the "commercial theatre" as the enemy it has always been?

I could go on, for he has been mixed up with the set's Glamor Girl, the murderer in the final incident, and people have warned him against her although they are no more explicit to him than I am here to the reader. Rivette would seem to have but one defensibly coherent message in all this: the milieu of Paris is one where fear of a certain kind has become a poison. Its grounds may have some general basis, some past basis perhaps, but by and large, fear here is the mental disease we know as paranoia; otherwise there would be no justification for keeping it a secret whether the deaths in the film are suicides or homicides, whether the grounds for fear are real or illusory, and whether the murderous Glamor Girl (whose nationality, by the way, is given as American) is a real foreign agent or a Paris-grown nut. I fancy she's a nut and that Rivette means to assay a moral poison in the Paris he fondly calls ours.

This same poison, I think, exists at Marienbad under the hypothetic brand name of a famous perfume. This stereo-scent spreads its magic amid the audience because Marienbad becomes, in Resnais' film, a high society bomb shelter protecting luxurious living from taking the future seriously. The Marienbad chateau, in history's full perpective, is close to the Versailles which it resembles—the Versailles from which its race of owners were forever driven. Never underestimate the cuteness of the French. Even peaceable Frenchmen (at times, like Caligari's somnambulist, without knowing it) may be placing plastiques full of perfume about the movie houses of the world. And the plastique may be (as *Paris Is Ours* would illustrate) a stink bomb with a slow burn. Rivette's film, full of common city sights and the arty, intellectualish, politically conscious set, is itself an insidiously prolonged stink

79

of suspicion; possibly a warning, possibly a nose-thumbing, possibly a lark, or possibly degrees of all three.

I believe it points, however deliberately, to the view that all is not right with the Paris edition of *Vogue* and that *Paris Soir* might change its policy too; not to mention *Match* with all its Bardottiness. I remind myself that in *Jules and Jim*, Catherine wants to read aloud Goethe's *Elective Affinities;* so the dialogue tells us and we see a copy of it. Well she might want to, poor girl, but she probably intuits the task would be useless considering the two male dopes she has to cope with. The fact is, the premises at the chalet needs only the presence of another woman, Jim's fiancée, to duplicate the situation in Goethe's novel. Everybody in *Elective Affinities*, however, is very well educated, and is apprised, before the action is over, just what an "elective affinity" is, and why. The "Jules" and the "Jims" will never know. In a way, that is partly what makes them attractive to Truffaut, to Catherine and to the audience. What a couple of precious prunes they are! Imagine quoting Baudelaire's opinion of women before a woman you want: a woman, moreover, who is likely to feel (I quote Jules) "unappreciated"! That first drop of Catherine's into the water should have been a fair warning to anybody but balmy, uneducated Bohemians that the second time she would take the man of her choice (seeing that he has balked) with her. And that is what she does. This is why the enlightened cannot believe in the interest, even if they must accept the physical datum, of Catherine's final act. Her men are too dumb to anticipate it, and no man with normal self-respect lets himself be as dumb as that—unless, of course, he's a character from *Paris Is Ours*, more specifically the one who lets a lady drive him out to the country and shoot him dead. I wonder how many of *those* there are?

80

Reality into Dream into
Myth into Charade into Dollars

An occasion comes when the film industry (there are no exceptions these days, even in France) feels freer than ever to invent, to exploit in a single stroke both its myth of technique and its myth of reality, on both of which it finds itself obliged to depend for existence. This occasion arises when it selects a theme of overt self-inspection, revealing certain processes of its make-believe and a modicum of the lasting, dreamlike effect produced by these processes on reality; that is, on the personalities of the actors. This was done in *A Star Is Born*, one of the earliest Technicolor features of the thirties; and even then the rudiments of the strange ritual were plain.

Not so many years ago, *A Star Is Born* was remade in a quite undistinguished version. The scene was still Hollywood, of course, the object still to provide a glamorous morality play concerning the awful damage which time may wreak on the fact and myth of personal success: that timeless entity of these centuries of individualism. This was also the theme of *Sunset Boulevard*, but in the thirties the theme was prospected with what straight good faith the movie people then were capable of, which was more than in the forties or the fifties. Ours is the day of candid-camera lowdowns as witnessed by *Life*, or a good proxy, and hence we got, in the epochal *Sunset Boulevard*, the sort of moral realism that is still capsuled in archly cryptic items about the stars' lives that are perennially pandered in gossip columns. The real film columnist, Hedda Hopper, is not on the telephone in the last moments of *Sunset Boulevard* for nothing.

As for the self-kibitz, it was nothing really new for Hollywood, least of all in the shape, as here, of farcing the personality of the female star. The same was done in the thirties, and by no means without fun, in *Bombshell*, so-called to suggest the effect of Jean Harlow on her hypnotized public. This film featured as background the Metro-Goldwyn-Mayer lot as *Sunset Boulevard* was due to feature the Paramount lot. In *Bombshell*, life was seen as a Hollywood Bowl of intimate charades, the whole being as aptly comic-strip as the adventures of Orphan Annie or Li'l Abner. It would be a small boon, at least, to say that the same were true of *Sunset Boulevard*. But the strategy of the bright boys who made it, Brackett and Wilder, was otherwise. One may observe in passing that all the world needed was television to help along the myth that Hollywood private lives could be brought, bag and baggage, into everyone's home.

The modern wrinkle was to do a nostalgic myth by hiring a once-great glamor girl, Gloria Swanson, and a once-great foreign director, Erich von Stroheim, to portray roles decidedly not themselves as they were circa *Sunset Boulevard*, but apparently genre types which, at least once, might have been carried to such extremes as those revealed in this film. On the other hand, so much is artifice supposed to have entered the Hollywood bloodstream, it is perhaps flattering to pretend that anything about the home industry is ever expected to be quite "real." If the American movies have a golden rule, it is this: The customers will swallow anything so long as it be done with enough punch and style. And what is punch and style in this particular case? The style, as always, is opulence (here documentary because of the actual professional background) and the punch is the spectacle of a one-time real star pretending that nowadays one-time real stars make scandalous fools of themselves and even shoot their unfaithful gigolos in the back.

If it was true in 1950, it was probably meant to be true now. Yet one opines that this allegation, on the corollary evidence, is, and was, false. Real murder has taken place within the professional colony of Hollywood as elsewhere in the world, but exactly because of this fact, discretion forbade that the rough stuff of *Sunset Boulevard* should bear any tangible resemblance to it. If, like the heroine, there are still ex-stars out there who cherish insanely pretentious delusions of making comebacks, one trusts that in private life they are more convincingly mad and amusing than Miss Swanson succeeds in being as Norma Desmond. Her really good moments (most of them pathetic) are wasted in a part which as an entity has neither authority nor finish—and from where, to be sure, could the "authority" have come? All that has authority in this film is the scale implicitly present in the ex-star's million dollars, and visible in her huge ornate house and swimming pool and the dozens of photographs of her decorating her living room. We have here one more way of reflecting the industrial power that is at the heart of the Hollywood scale. Was all this, as the kindest commentators suggested, tongue-in-cheek satire? Scarcely; since the actress legend was all too realistically framed by the documentary saga of an ambitious young script-writer, whose hard luck has guided him spank into Miss Desmond's lonely arms; result: tainted romance.

The Paramount lot, as I say, is literally present in *Sunset Boulevard*. Furthermore, by some odd coincidence, Miss Swanson, when she worked steady during the twenties, was a Paramount star, and Cecil de Mille (shown directing *Samson and Delilah,* which he did direct) made Miss Swanson's biggest pictures, in the old days, and made them for Paramount. Stars may come and go, fashions certainly change, and farce may contract open liaison with a morality play, but business goes on (*i.e.*, hopefully) as usual; all the better, one may infer, if it is kept in the family. The romance of the subplot is bred right in the Paramount script department, where a young woman anxious to write film stories entices the gigolo away from his dishonor to assist her when the rest of the studio lot is dark. True love blossoms despite hell and the climax comes when the anxious ex-star, checking up on those nights out, discovers all and spills the facts to the young lady over the phone. Angry script-writer-gigolo leaves ex-star precipitately: bang-bang!

An elaborate mad-scene, in which the lady imagines she is acting in a new film triumph and not walking downstairs to be carried off to jail, was the socko finish to this very gaudy tale. If there was the least common sense to it, it was the sadistic common sense of the audience: all in all the most dependable factor present. Most audiences derive a profane joy, I daresay, from seeing wealth and fame end up with the wrong end of the stick. The special moral of the script-writer-gigolo's end may have been harder for the fans to savor. The efflorescence of the young man's conscience, when he strips off the expensive baubles with which he has been showered and denounces his corrupter, is (besides being lugubriously and unintentionally funny) one of the most callous and tasteless scenes I remember ever to have seen anywhere. It was amazing to find, even in the movies, self-conscious masculine virtue so thick-skinned, childish and mechanical—grotesquely stupid, indeed, for only a ham-headed goon would not have anticipated that shot in the back after insulting a half-crazy mistress and packing his bags—considering that, at the moment and conspicuously, a little revolver nestled nervously in her hands. But perhaps the movie public felt that the gentleman in question, having been such a traitor to decent manhood, deserved his unparalleled stupidity.

Of course, I doubt that anyone could be found lurking in Hollywood, now or yesterday, willing to testify that life as shown in *Sunset Boulevard* is anything, at bottom, but a clean, wholesome, money-making scheme. However, a shrewd enough resident might suggest that the real factual pertinence of the movie lay in its being a satiric obituary for the star system, which has been very unwell for the last quarter of a century. The strongest survivor in the vamp style was Garbo, who went and apparently won't ever come back. The foreign director, too, insofar as he hasn't been assimilated, is in disfavor, and Von Stroheim was notorious for never having been properly naturalized in Hollywood. Playing the ex-star's ex-husband—now, and still worshipfully, her butler—Von Stroheim provides a caricature of himself at his worst, the operetta-style Prussian officer, but so paradoxically grim here that he manages to seem like nothing so much as an undertaker who has missed his calling.

Yet both Miss Swanson and Mr. Von Stroheim, as workers who in the past gave Hollywood long and valiant service, were suitably rewarded here in the twilight of their careers. The home industry is never averse to posing as a

83

charitable institution with more imagination and cash than a home for retired actors. It is plain, moreover, that the insistence on the documentary angle in *Sunset Boulevard* produced a quasi-Pirandellian brand of illusionist realism, which the industry is destined, I hazard, never to get out of its system. Observe the naked elements of the case: A real ex-star who has never quite faded—according to her repeated comebacks—is climactically hired to impersonate a fictitious ex-star who *has* quite faded, automatically disproving, thus, the film's obvious slant that undying glamor psychology leads surely to disaster. No mechanical self-contradiction, this, but the calculated whirligig of the charade-minded movies at its dumbest and dizziest. Instead of holding a charity benefit for Gloria, they asked her to work for her money—and made more than a few honest dollars for themselves.

84

The Dream-Amerika of Kafka and Chaplin

Had Kafka never written at all his fragmentary novel, *Amerika,* and accordingly a critic had suggested, on the basis of the other two novels, that if naturalistically inflected, the saga of his hero, K., might well make use of the European myth of "America," one can imagine the murmur of skepticism that a certain school of opinion would have exhaled as to the probability of such an event. And yet Kafka did write *Amerika,* he did export his epic hero to the shores of this country and subject him, in deliberately Dickensian manner, to the hazards of a young modern civilization, ending, as customarily, on an ambiguous note, but this time of hope rather than of despair. It has been pointed out that Kafka was not so Dickensian as he imagined, and indeed, far from taking Dickens' satirical slant on this country, he merely put it in the line of those homes of bureaucratic mechanism and economic hazard that appear as "Continental" entities in *The Castle* and *The Trial.*

Inevitably, Kafka merely extended the vision of his self-hero and his spiritual adventure by taking him to something so identifiable as the Statue of Liberty and, finally, to Oklahoma. Max Brod reports that Kafka found light-hearted pleasure in speaking to his friends of his hero, Karl Rossmann. One cannot help feeling that in recognizing K. as an immigrant to an identifiable "foreign country," and having him seek there an ordinary job like anyone else, Kafka was to displace his hero, K., to a purely figurative dilemma from what had been a realistic one; he was producing a *conte* in the old-fashioned sense, a tale of temptation and adventure, innocence and world-wickedness.

This procedure, of course, did not deflect Kafka's peculiar drive toward the statement of his situation. In making his protagonist, Karl, so young, K.'s master seemed, at the same time, to be relinquishing in advance the subjectivity of his intellectual and moral world. In substance, he converted his own personal myth, with its European constriction and metaphoric girth (the "fairy tale" land of *The Castle*), into a common myth with a legendary openness, America itself, land of two writers he admired, Benjamin Franklin and Walt Whitman, land of physical girth and job opportunities.

It seems most significant that, as his biographer, Brod, reports, Kafka could gleefully recite to his friends the beginning of *Amerika*. There was something of an unburdening, no doubt, in sending his little hero off to a real country; something *comic* in visualizing him sighting from the sea, like hundreds of thousands of other Europeans, the Statue of Liberty—her arm oddly, in *Amerika,* holding aloft a *sword*. Kafka was dealing with a *pre-existent* myth of a strange land, though one testable only in the imagination; if his hero was to remain indelibly his (as though his body were branded somewhere with Kafka's fatal initial), he also entered a domain astonishingly similar to the one braved by Charles Chaplin's real and fictitious "immigrant."

Kafka wrote his novel, strangely enough, at the same time that Charles Chaplin was molding his theatrical fortune in this country, having arrived from England in 1910. The date of publication of the first chapter of *Amerika* is 1913, the year that Chaplin's vaudeville act, with which he had been touring the States, attracted the notice of Hollywood; the following year, he was making comedies for Mack Sennett. Though actually, like the immigrant Karl Rossmann, Chaplin was a young man seeking to make his way in life, the motley he first assumed for the movies was that of his vaudeville "turn." It was the stock villain, inherited from the Victorian era, in dress suit and top hat and with walrus mustache. However, Chaplin's now traditional character, Charlie, soon emerged: a boy in charade as a man.

Where innumerable young male immigrants are involved, why should Kafka's "Karl" and Chaplin's "Charlie" be worthy of special comparison? The most obvious reason has been noted by other commentators: the general resemblance of the plot of *Amerika* to the plots of Chaplin comedies. There is no question of "derivation," yet that makes the parallelism all the more important; Karl and Charlie the Tramp are heroes of the identical international myth: the great adventure of the young foreigner coming head-on to the United States to start a new life and hoping to rise to a level beyond any available to him in his native land. In the real-life dimension, this was literally Chaplin's career; he was, of course, already a professional when he landed, but a very modest one: he succeeded here more quickly and more grandly than he had dared to hope. Karl Rossmann's uncle, Senator Edward Jacob, is himself the successful immigrant made over according to the Land-of-opportunity legend. Yet in two years' time, Chaplin had evolved his farce-villain into a comic picaro, the daydreaming "Tramp," perennially destined to be the economic dregs and chivalrously to pursue true love in vain. Thus from the purely economic angle, Chaplin's character enacted the moral history of Kafka's K., never able to climb the ladder of success to economic security and professional orthodoxy and never able to extricate himself from the suspicion of crime, of being an "undesirable." Thus we see that the "undesirable alien" familiar to the history of this country, and typified by Charlie the Tramp, is the correlative in actual life of K., the fictitious "undesirable alien" of Kafka's Castle-land.

86

It cannot pass as insignificant that so many of the inventions of Chaplin's comedies, first to last, relate so closely to inventions in *Amerika*. Karl Ross-mann is a servant girl's bastard while Charlie's origin is appropriately obscure, being hinted indirectly only later on in one of Chaplin's masterpieces, *The Kid,* where the baby picked up by the Tramp in an alley is also illegitimate. Karl has a box and umbrella that correspond to Charlie's standard wardrobe; the cane and the bundle. Karl's articles are mislaid and returned; by curious chance, a film known as, among other titles, *Charlie and the Umbrella* (1914), features "a misunderstanding all around as to the ownership of an umbrella."[1] Karl's uncle, when he first appears, carries a "bamboo cane." This quasi-weapon (Charlie often fought with his cane) is suggested by the sword replacing Liberty's torch in Kafka's novel. What can this mean but that a certain degree of sheer *force* is required to succeed in the country which Karl is entering? Karl's struggle with the bureaucracy begins on board ship where a roughhouse of farce-comedy inflection takes place. Chaplin's immigrant role came in 1917 and he is involved in complicated business with a coin in a restaurant, just as is Karl after joining the vagabonds, Delamarche and Robinson, and going to a restaurant with them. Charlie's coin falls through a hole in his pocket; Karl's money is hidden in his clothes lining, where he surreptitiously has to dig for it.

There is no deep symbolism about these casual parallels. Indeed, they are interesting if merely because they point to the framing situation of the two immigrant heroes, but such inventions still are not mere logical parallels in a common situation; in turn, they relate to the sensibilities of the two artists responsible for them, one mutually illuminating the other. If Charlie can be seen in Karl, and Karl in Charlie, the fact suggests a higher relationship between their creators; by happy coincidence, the very names of the heroes are equivalents, and in one sense it seems obvious that Karl is nothing but Kafka's "Charlie."

To continue the parallel of fictive elements: Karl's perpetual run-in with the authorities is in line with Charlie's mishaps on his recurrent jobs; equally, Karl and Charlie obtain good jobs only for fate to play them some trick so that they find themselves "on the road" once more and in disgrace. Karl is not unintelligent as Charlie is not unrefined; but their very sensitivity and dignity are misunderstood, are the very traits which help most effectively to render them outcasts. Karl is unwarrantably tumbled out of his Uncle Edward's patronage because of an oblique personal "betrayal," one of those little affairs judged with blind bureaucratic arrogance. In Charlie's perpetual saga, the equivalent of Karl's uncle is the dipsomaniac millionaire of *City Lights,* who befriends him while drunk only to repudiate him when sober. Where an arbitrary ethic operates in Kafka's story, a Dionysian vice prevails in Chaplin's. But the *arbitrariness* of the adult patron's behavior, in each case, is the signifying factor in relation to Karl's and Charlie's innocence and helplessness. Uncle Edward, Mr. Pollunder, and Mr. Green form a triumvirate of fat, cigar-smoking "capitalists" that correspond directly to the type as found in Chaplin's comedies.

[1] *An Index to the Films of Charles Chaplin,* by Theodore Huff (page 4).

In my book on Chaplin, I traced the pattern of partnership with an older man throughout the comedian's artistic life. The same theme occurs in *Amerika* at the very beginning when Karl encounters the ship's stoker; the purely intellectual aggressiveness and moral precocity of Karl is emphasized because here it is he who tries to help the stoker out of a jam, rather than vice versa. Yet this is precisely the situation when Big Jim, the gold-mine prospector in *The Gold Rush,* gets knocked on his head, loses his memory, and has to employ Charlie's aid in locating his rich claim; by being "unwitted," the older man becomes dependent on Charlie's "dim wit" and yet stalwart, loyal spirit.

The parallels strangely interlace. The vagabonds, Delamarche and Robinson, men "young" but definitely older than Karl (a "European intermediate pupil"), pick Karl up in order to take him along to "the gold fields of the West," or mythologically speaking, California. It is typical that, even at the optimistic finale of *Amerika,* its hero gets only as far as Oklahoma, but still Karl has been in the company of two "adult patrons" however irresponsible; actually it is *they* who are to exploit *him.* Scenically, it is easy to see why Kafka's and Chaplin's "Amerika"s are so much akin. Both are largely legendary, "theatrical," and for reasons perhaps more complex than at first may appear.

Since Kafka did not know America save from literary accounts, he visualizes it much as a spectator might, as a sort of "theater"; consequently, the device of the "Nature Theatre of Oklahoma," an actual theatrical project which finally absorbs Karl as one of its employees, acquires an inevitability of its own. It is the metaphoric figure for all America as visually anticipated by those naïve ones still separated from it by an ocean: the Land of Opportunity as a stage setting presided over by "female" angels raised high above the ground. The commedia dell' arte vein of Chaplin's farces gave an artificial feeling to whatever was identifiably American in his films. In sum, Kafka's "Amerika" is reciprocally telescoped by Chaplin's. It is a land of phantasmal mechanisms (Klaus Mann once noted that the elaborate desk in the house of Karl's uncle resembles a trick affair in a Chaplin comedy), riotous saloons, millionaires and servants, complicated mechano-organisms such as hotels, mad activities like political rallies, and the lurking threat of the policeman (especially allergic to an immigrant). Karl has a nightmarish vision of a "telegraphists' hall" that suggests, both psychologically and mechanically, certain sequences in *Modern Times.* One passage in *Amerika* can be called positively cinematic; it describes a panoramic impression of Karl's while in New York: ". . . there opened out on both sides an endless perspective of pavements filled with a moving mass of people, slowly shuffling forward, whose singing was more homogeneous than that of any single human voice." This might be an actual excerpt from a synopsis meant to indicate montage effects of audio-visual nature: superimposed marchers with vocal chorus and music.

The atmosphere of Mr. Pollunder's great house, described as "a fortress not a mansion," has the *chinoiserie* of "mystery houses" on the screen and something of the tone of Hearst's legendary dwelling as parodied by Orson Welles in *Citizen Kane.* In this house, Karl is treated to jiu-jitsu by Pollunder's athletic daughter, who almost knocks him backward out of a window, a most familiar incident in the hurly-burly of Charlie's physical career. This episode also affords a striking instance of the cruel disillusionment so typical of Charlie's erotic fate. Karl's wrestling with Clara Pollunder has already hinted of Charlie's combats with hefty dames (for example, Marie Dressler), and late that night, when it would seem the erotic intimation of their struggle is about to be carried out in Clara's bedroom, the girl asks Karl to play the piano; music then seems designed as the sentimental prelude to their stolen happiness. But suddenly Karl hears applause from the next room, the connecting door is opened, and beyond it Clara's fiancé is discovered sitting in bed; obviously, Karl realizes, the two already sleep together, and he has been made a dupe by the young man, who could find no other way than this to induce Karl to play for him. In the etiology of Kafka's symbolism, this incident no doubt has a rather complex meaning, but its parallel in Charlie's history embodied but one hard, ineluctible fact: monotonously crushing disappointments in the Tramp's idyllic dream of love.

Certain details of pure invention by Kafka suggest the very tone and style of Chaplin's inventions; conspicuous is the behavior of a sleeping man in a dormitory which Karl visits: every time the man breathes, his legs and arms elevate themselves from the bed; also, we see the disreputable Robinson, after a drunken debauch, extravagantly swathed in bandages as a practical joke. It is precisely these literal resemblances which point the *difference* between the intellectual tone of Kafka's comedy and that of Chaplin's; on the other hand, do not such things, as well as the aggregate of these parallels, indicate an essential brotherhood between Karl and Charlie?

One of the most remarkable stylistic traits of Kafka's art is the total barrenness therein of the *mood* of sentiment. Karl, and even K., have what might be categorically called "sexual relations" and "love scenes"; a certain shy, reluctant will, however, characterizes Karl's erotic impulses. It is an ambivalence of sensory taste; he shrinks physically from Clara and seems to disdain contact with Therese, the forlorn "servant-girl type" with whom he forms a friendship as Charlie used to do with luckless female workers. Karl's reunion with Fanny, posing as an angel outside the Nature Theatre of Oklahoma, is jocular and comradely, not sentimental or intense. The "manic" quality of the dénouement of *Amerika,* analyzed by Paul Goodman, lies in the general atmosphere rather than in anything intimate or personal. Charlie, for his part, has a "manic fit" of truer character when, in *The Kid,* all his troubles disappear in an ecstatic dream of heaven, where he disports himself on wings with a girl-angel. Charlie is invariably sentimental, even exquisite, with his girl friends, but the element uniting the erotics of the two heroes, like the arbitrariness of behavior by the rich adult patron, is an almost inexplicable *barrier,* signified usually by Charlie's humiliated awareness of his inferiority; he is loved in return, sometimes, but the substance of the Tramp's legend is alienation from sexual happiness—as was significantly enough expounded in the dénouement of *Monsieur Verdoux*. The principle of alienation just as accurately defines K.'s, if not also Karl's, position with regard to women. The maternal symbol appears twice in *Amerika*, as the "Manageress" of the hotel and as the stout but "beautiful" opera singer, so much like a schoolboy's fantasy and worshiped by Delamarche and Robinson; Karl, however, rejects the singer, thus implicitly refusing to "find his mother" in her.

If Karl's sexual future seems happy and secure by token of the isolated and imperfect climax of *Amerika*, Charlie's seems the opposite by token of the climactic film, *Monsieur Verdoux*, assuming that we may regard Charlie's story as an unbroken continuity. By token of Verdoux, Charlie is changed, however, and has the bitter, ironic inflection which corresponds to K., hero of the pessimistic fables, *The Castle* and *The Trial*. The latter, like *Monsieur Verdoux*, ends in the execution of its hero as a criminal. Verdoux is mature, sophisticated, having risen to success and fallen; thus he is not the "Charlie" of Chaplin's prolonged tale of the picaro. But, like K., Verdoux has secreted an innate weakness, a flaw that brings about his downfall; if he has succeeded temporarily he has done so as an opportunist and a swindler, one of whose weapons is murder; likewise (like Charlie so often), Verdoux has been a masquerader, a charlatan. So the principal difference between Karl and K. is exactly that between Charlie and Verdoux: one of the two in both pairs is essentially *innocent*, the other essentially *guilty*.

Verdoux's "Europe" is K.'s "Europe" with the ambitious French bank clerk succeeding by dishonesty, by a defiant plot against established authority. As we know, K. refused to use illicit means throughout the two parts of his story, *The Castle* and *The Trial*. Charlie, naturally innocent as Karl is, will not—even if only because he cannot—use such means. Charlie's "dishonesty" is strictly defensive, his flight from the law substantially the result of a "technical misunderstanding." With odd identicality, Karl is pursued back and forth through city streets by a policeman in *Amerika* even as countless times Charlie was chased through the endless purlieus of his comedies. If Charlie is guilty of some chance misdemeanor, it is no more than that of a homeless "juvenile delinquent"; all that he needs to "reform" him is "normal conditions," security, and self-confidence, so that he can "grow up" properly. Of the scene of *Amerika*, Max Brod writes: "In enigmatic language Kafka used to hint smilingly that within this "almost limitless" theatre his young hero was going to find again a profession, a stand-by, his freedom, even his old home and his parents, as if by some celestial witchery."

Something of this same feeling, albeit sentimentalized, permeates Chaplin's story of the infant waif succored by the Tramp in *The Kid*. There is no question but that, in this film, Chaplin in some sense was reviving his own youth as an urchin on London streets, a fatherless boy who doubtless longed for a male parent. Chaplin's "kid" finds his real mother and a foster father (Charlie himself). This search for the lost parents is extant in *Amerika* but unsuccessful in the unfinished novel, while it is overlaid by allegory in the other works of Kafka.

Brod, as quoted just above, was referring, of course, exclusively to the hero of *Amerika*. Nothing in Chaplin's comedies, analogously, refers to the history of Verdoux's youth, except as we can imagine it like Charlie's given a dissident inflection. But in the sense of *artistic* origins, Verdoux does have an early background; it lies, strangely enough, in his famous "variety" act and the first quasi-villains of his pristine days in Hollywood. In these one-reel films, Chaplin is seen as a burlesque of the dude portrayed in *Monsieur Verdoux;* the mustaches are pointed, formal clothes that fit are usually present. Like "Desperate Desmond" of the old American comic strip—a clear vestige of Victorianism —Charlie's comedy villain is a degradation into ham melodrama. In the epoch-making *Tillie's Punctured Romance,* the youthful face of the Tramp emerges with unique and transient clarity; the mustaches are now smaller, neat, divided coquettishly in the middle; they are the hirsute ornament of a good-looking young dandy, echoed later by the mature dandy of Verdoux and close to the boulevard comedian of Max Linder, who inspired Chaplin to emulation. This Chaplin villain, however comically, created disorder through willful design; not more or less inadvertently, as did Charlie the "prop man" and Karl the "lift operator." The early, heavy-mustached villain is a home-wrecker even as Verdoux is; so in this latest version of his protagonist, Chaplin undertakes a conscious malice, and taking leave of Charlie's ill-fated innocence, assumes a conscious guilt.

A great deal has been written of the motives and character of Kafka's guilt as mirrored in the mythical quandaries of his hero, K. The guilt in *The Trial* is taken for granted; it is preëmptive, beyond choice. The problem which K. cannot dispose of is the role of his *consciousness* in assuming guilt and so meriting punishment. Metaphysically—here is the redemptive aura of his fiction— he is guiltless; the obscure arena where he meets death from the two executioners is the abstract and subjective realm of self-condemnation for a crime, of which "technically" he is guilty, if only because of the pain that has been equivalent to a punishment, but which (even as Oedipus!) he did not "knowingly" commit. Whatever misadventures Charlie the Tramp endures must be observed as having this same subjective innocence and objective guilt. There is the epic incident in *Modern Times* when he picks up a danger flag fallen from the back of a truck, finds himself at the head of a demonstration of radicals, is arrested as their leader and thrown in jail. And in *The Great Dictator,* there is the "crime" of being a Jew. In terms of moral consciousness, on the other hand, how curiously, precisely inverse are Chaplin's Charlie and Kafka's K.! Charlie knows what he is (or does) but cannot be aware of anything as a crime. K. is very much aware of *a* crime but he cannot identify *what* crime he has committed.

The inverse parallelism extends to the relation between the remaining members of the two pairs: Verdoux knows what he does and it is *guiltily* done; Karl also knows what he does but it is *innocently* done. Chaplin posits guilt for his

91

fictive hero through real moral action (Verdoux's schemes), *innocence* for him through the subjective ambiguity of symbolic action (Charlie's dream life). Kafka does the reverse: the real moral action of *Karl* establishes his innocence, whereas the symbolic action of *K.'s* subjectively ambiguous world establishes his guilt.

The position of illusion, the artistic symbol, rendered by the Nature Theatre of Oklahoma, is succinct in *Amerika;* the imaginative goal, the "aesthetic object," can be attained only through a genuine, clear-headed innocence such as that of Karl Rossmann. If guilt adulterates the total consciousness of a man, it places the imaginative goal, of which the Castle is also a symbol, beyond reach, and art can represent only the tortuous antechambers to the sanctity of that goal. The sentimental waif Charlie always lived in *his* "nature theater," it was a world of comic plunge and reversal projected from his own innocent imagination: compact with the hobgoblins and hidden traps of "reality." When the Tramp awoke from his doorstep dream, he found himself "Verdoux," a part of "the system," part of an urbanization of the "nature theater," the arena of ruthless profit and loss; here, he could only carry out logically the lurking villainy of the "social leper." When Chaplin's misfit "hero" became too practical, he reverted to the misfit "villain," now armed with a conscious moral apology (Verdoux's witness-stand and death-cell speeches).

The most significant thing seems to be that Chaplin's hero—Verdoux or Charlie—is always in a kind of *flight*. He turns his back on his situation; innocent or guilty, he prepares for a sudden departure, he vacates, he runs away or shuffles off as we saw Charlie do so often, his silhouette growing smaller in the distance. It is not for nothing that it is M. Verdoux's *back* we see last in the latest film; all that he "faces" is death. Kafka's superiority as a man seems to be that he was always "facing" everything: life in one chunk ahead of him. Whether it is K. dying by the executioners' knives or Karl climbing toward Fanny on her aerial pedestal, one feels the farewell steadiness of a direct, open, frontal gaze—never the back view, however depressing (Verdoux) or pathetic (Charlie). Karl leaves his post as lift operator and later is punished with dismissal, but through his defection he has *faced* a higher moral obligation: humanity toward a fellow creature.

Yet finally it is the weight and definition of a *scene* which brings together Karl and Charlie under the roof of the same world. In whatever moral or physical stance we may leave the Chaplinesque or the Kafkan hero, we sense around him the strange, by no means reassuring, atmosphere of a "World's Fair," an often shocking polyglot of art and reality, a "theater of action" containing castles and courtrooms, nature and machines, love and murder, jobs and joblessness, the innocent inextricably fused with the guilty, and youth making its dreamlike way; in other words: a fantasy "Amerika" that we find difficult to keep separate from the real one.

III

THE
CULT

more or less refined

Hollywood as a Universal Church

If it were stated as a thesis that Hollywood is indifferent to everything but the personal-professional triumph, and that therefore it constitutes (since its influence is virtually limitless) a Universal Church of professionalism, with Money as the presiding deity, that thesis might be called "obvious." On the other hand, it might be flatly contradicted by those who admire, or at least take seriously, the films of social purpose, the "problem pictures." For aren't these films "about something"—something contemporary, close, and verifiable in terms of facts existing beyond Hollywood's doors?

My answer is "Yes!" But what determines their true content is neither the statistics which inhere in them nor the ostensible message of social toleration which they carry like a picket sign, but rather the precise inflections of their plots and the form inevitably given them by various Hollywood prejudices and conventions. I intend to marshal first a number of general facts which are well enough known by some, but which, when taken in relation to the perspective of the problem films, assume a new edge and importance, and reveal thereby the tacit presence of what may be dubbed Hollywood's "Higher Creed." The reader is asked therefore to be patient while, preliminarily, certain basic ground is surveyed.

A single fact permeates the background of commercial film in the United States. Professional society in Hollywood is a cohesive group in which the *unit* does not emerge as an "individual" until his name appears in letters of a certain height and thickness and placement—and stays that way. The resulting internal snobbery means that social gatherings and the standards observed therein are dominated precisely by size of salary, and "culture" is thus unequivocally equated with money. Not that purely social cliques are nonexistent. They exist, assuredly, but are dominated exclusively by top professionals.

A prime theme of Hollywood for many years, we may note, has been the success story, and especially the internal success story—that of theatrical talent on stage and screen. The dramatic resources of such film stories have been limited, naturally, both by standard taboos and by the narrow material usually

95

chosen. One thing has been easy and frequent: to show that the road to success is hard, and that even when fame and fortune are achieved by the individual, his bed may be expensive but not all of roses. This formula has been applied at large, of course, to all professional groups; to the Vernon Castles and Pasteur, John L. Sullivan and assorted aviation pioneers, George M. Cohan and the Curies, Bell and Gershwin, Zola and Al Jolson. Moreover, there has been the garden variety of success epic, usually about fictitious composers or showgirls (for example, the mythologically conscious *Ziegfield Girl*).

The recent inflections of this archetype have actual precedents not altogether without implications of social prejudice. While anti-Semitism as such did not hamper John Garfield in his roles as the violinist in *Humoresque* or the prize fighter in *Body and Soul,* no secret was made of his national origin; indeed, what may be called his "race" served well to accent, however implicitly, his rise if not also his fall. Such tacitness in the studios operates the more forcefully in those biographic romances where, as with Al Jolson (two installments) and Gershwin, the Jewish hero is a resounding celebrity of real life. Wherever professional snobbery might have operated against singer or composer on the rise, prejudice as a factor was excluded simply because of the secure truth that the theater, especially Hollywood and the musical-comedy stage, has long been democratically open to whoever could make the grade—"regardless of race, creed, or color."

For us in the United States, the world of professional entertainment is an economic democracy where the artistic product ("entertainment") is without true ethical responsibility, and the human objective is profit and nothing more. Society at large is less particular about those who *entertain* it than about those it *receives at home.* This is mostly because stage and screen are realms of make-believe, of masquerade, where—to begin with—the rule for general purposes is for the Jewish entertainer, on every but the highest artistic level, to forget or disguise his Jewishness. In passing, two monumental facts should be explicitly recorded: First, nose operations may be *de rigueur* where topflight success is concerned, and are commonly desirable in lay life; and, second, religion is taboo in Hollywood stars' publicity.

The argument for Hollywood standards as a strong democratic force might be thought, offhand, well based, because of the very conditions I have been describing. But what is the formal mode of this "democratic force" which creates universal criteria for noses, manners, and acting talent? It is monolithic and hierarchic with only a slight modification of uniformity. This modification is a dualism derived from comic values, symbolic evil, and old age; this means that screen stories require, no less than "heroes" and "heroines," character actors, deep-dyed villains, and comedians, the last of whom may have outrageous noses and be geniuses of clumsiness. At the same time, even comedians appear in the mufti of private life, and to a certain extent, if famous enough, they even have "glamor"; thus, we must assume that comedians also may develop the drawing-room manners of a Fredric March (who, after all, can in

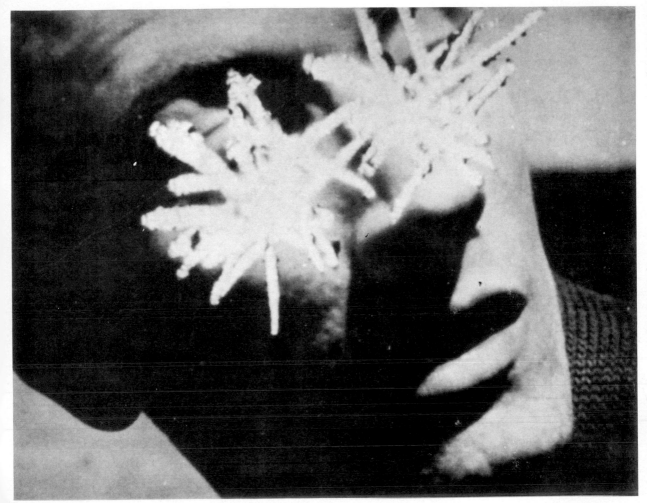

Reflections on Black (Brakhage)

The Dream

The chief imaginative trend among Experimental or avant-garde film-makers is action as a *dream* and the actor as a *somnambulist*. This film shot employs actual scratching on the reel to convey the magic of seeing while "dreaming awake"; the world in view becomes that of poetic action pure and simple: action without the restraints of single-level consciousness, everyday reason, and so-called realism. Dangers of excess and other errors lurk in this sphere of artistic freedom, but it is the one inevitable road of true creation in cinema and can be applied—as in the film from which this shot was taken—to common human experience as well as to the "exotica" of pathology and supernaturalism. As proven by the brilliant commercial film, *Dead of Night*, these "exotica" become, in any case, the common human experience of the thrill-addicted movie-goer.

Cesare, the somnambulist of *The Cabinet of Dr. Caligari,* has been an arch symbol for subsequent avant-garde film-making, one of whose heroines is seen below. Art is the action which knits the passive dreamer, as it knits the passive spectator, to realms of experience beyond his conscious and unconscious control. In such realms, wild excitement is often found by way of the movies. But rarely, except in avant-garde films, does the strict pulse of beauty govern the engines of "wild excitement."

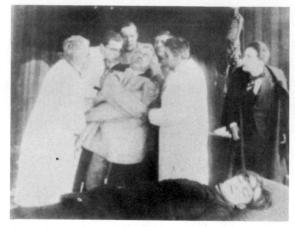

The Cabinet of Dr. Caligari
Courtesy Gideon Bachmann

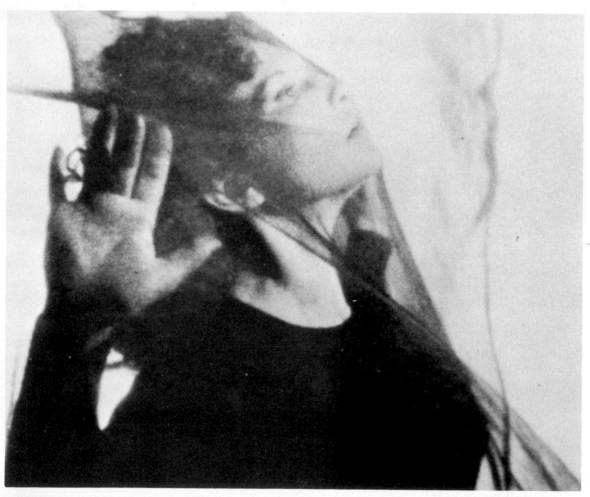

Meshes of the Afternoon (Deren-Hammid)

Courtesy Maya Deren

Movement for its own sake, as in the Action Melodrama, is a special madness of the commercial film. On this page, however, are vivid examples of the mobile technique used aesthetically to create a dimension of movement in still sculpture, and an extra dimension of movement for a dancer by successive replacements of the scene through which he dances. All such devices, evoking a super-real plane of movement, aspire to that magic freedom of action which is characteristic of dreams.

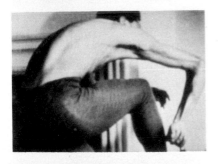

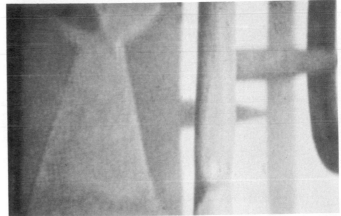

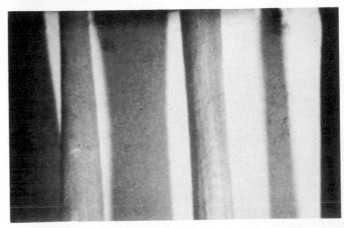

Study in Choreography for Camera (Deren)
Courtesy Maya Deren

Visual Variations on Noguchi (Menken)

Courtesy Cinema 16

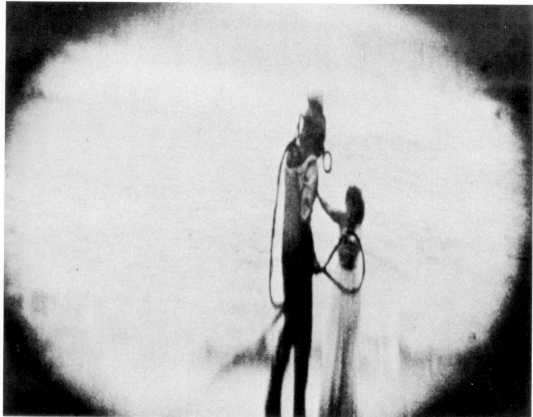

The Lead Shoes (Peterson)

Anamorphic photography (vertical or horizontal compression of image by special lenses) is a device for creating dreamlike illusions. Its aesthetic value is accurately suggested by comparing the woman and the deepsea diver, as they appear here anamorphically, with the location shot, where the "eyewitness" camera has recorded them. The plastic tension of this particular anamorphic shot acquires further interest by comparison with a very similar image by Eisenstein (above): the normal horizontal figure is "passive" while the anamorphic vertical is "active"; both are highly evocative of mood.

The Lead Shoes (location still)

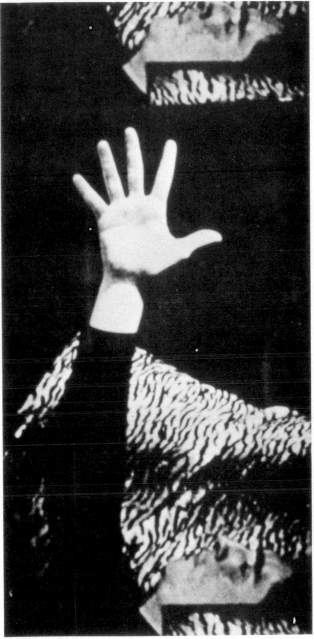

The hand as plastic symbol and "dancer" has had a distinct role in the annals of avant-garde film. The world's most ancient artists, who painted on the walls of pre-historic caves, were aware of the hand as an instrument of magic power at once empirical and symbolic. The horizontal "dreamer" of the avant-garde film does not forget this primordial reality; on the contrary, he resurrects it as an immediate visual presence, as his own eidolon of organic beauty.

Hand Written (Boultenhouse)
Courtesy Cinema 16

Prehistoric Hand (Castillo, Spain)
Courtesy Cinema 16

Alphaville (Godard)   Courtesy Pathé Contemporary Films

Alphaville (Godard)   Courtesy Pathé Comtemporary Films

Opposite are stills from Jean-Luc Godard's *Alphaville*, shown at the
Third New York Film Festival: this playful myth of the future, devoted
to the comic-strip cult of Pop Art, is a dry travesty aimed at reviving
sophisticated taste through puerile means. Note how the girl splayed against
the wall recalls the anti-gravitational passage of Orpheus to the Underworld
in Cocteau's film of 1950; also, how much the bit of Space Age fantasy
below it suggests the dreamy candle pattern of the still (elsewhere in this book)
from *Ivan the Terrible*. The plastic art of film, foolishly parodied though it be,
tends to survive. Yet modern styles (see below) tend to substitute documented
spontaneity and its "accidents" for calculated formal design such as the overlapping
faces from Resnais' film. Dream and reality are equally explosive; the problem
is to control them both.

Last Year At Marienbad (Resnais)   *Courtesy Astor Pictures*

Shadows (Cassavetes)   *Courtesy Lion International Films*

The Mirage (Weiss)

The Mirage (Weiss)

One of the most recent and ambitious efforts in the realm of the avant-garde is a Swedish film whose hero, shown here going "dance-crazy" from hunger, emulates our century's greatest interpreter of the hallucinated under-dog, Charlie Chaplin. This new hero also de-monstrates the important link between Chaplin's tramp and Kafka's hero, K., who wanders amid the chaos of great cities. In fact, the above glimpse of industry's "daymarish" labyrinth, with its cement-doused worker, illustrates the very spirit of Kafka's novel, *Amerika*.

turn impersonate Mr. Hyde); and if physically a comedian is too much unsuited to a role of romantic lover in real life, he may—like Jimmy (Snozzola) Durante —bob his nose a little.

If we are to conclude, as seems inevitable, that Hollywood's standards set up an internal convention perpetually refining itself toward universality, the instance of Danny Kaye offers a very particular import. Here is a comedian "resembling life" as much as did Harold Lloyd, who was the most normal-looking of the outstanding silent-screen comics. Both are Jewish and both achieved the big-time; both have exploited a semipathological awkwardness, primarily of sexual origin. But in Kaye's case one will note that he has an especially flashy personality and is a whiz (as seen in *Up in Arms*) at impersonation. A nightclub "emcee" rather than a clown, Kaye began his career in the Borscht Belt and, without getting permanently into costume or devising a genre manner, climbed to a command performance before English royalty and a visit with Bernard Shaw.

Kaye seems to illustrate the very pith of social-professional success in a handicapped person who has overcome his liability (perhaps stuttering or girl-shyness, or both, as elements of his routine indicate) by inverting it into an asset. Does anyone stop to consider that Kaye is Jewish? I hazard that many Jews do, and that his triumphant caterwauls echo intimately in many a breast in his audiences, especially in that of someone as personable as he, who hopes it is as short a step to Broadway as Kaye's film, *The Kid from Brooklyn,* demonstrates.

We have in Hollywood, then, in or out of mufti, nothing less than a Universal Church absorbing both Jewry and Christianity by means of a rigid social-professional creed. Yet, as we have seen recently, social reality has brought about an external modification of the monolithism: an explicit recognition of the "race prejudice" which, with respect to Jews, is so irrelevant in the social strongholds of professionalism. There have been five important commercial films on this theme: *Crossfire, Gentleman's Agreement, Home of the Brave, Lost Boundaries,* and *Pinky.* The idea that Hollywood should even *seem* to take sides in such large issues as social prejudices against Negroes and Jews was so shocking that the desire to exploit the commercial opportunity has not prevented big-time movie producers from begging off indirectly by insistence on the internal creed. In fact, except for a fresh opportunity to spread the professional doctrine, the producers would not have considered doing films on these public moral issues. Let us see what light may be thrown on this point by an analysis of these films.

It was a "natural" for John Garfield to take the part of the race victim in *Gentleman's Agreement.* Having been typed as rugged and sympathetic, rather than refined or handsome, his face was just right for that of the deserving underdog. And who is the gentile hero who finally takes up Garfield's cause? No one but Gregory Peck, correspondingly typed as handsome and noble, thus overwhelmingly ideal as the "Aryan" movie hero. What happens? Peck starts out by impersonating Jewishness (in name only) in order to write a series of

97

feature articles for a well-known magazine. Thus we do not see humiliated, eventually and somewhat ludicrously, a *real* Jew but a *charade* Jew. Through this odd initiation rite, Hollywood spares the real Jew until, as Garfield, he has gentile Peck in there punching for him. We hardly need Peck's masquerading girl secretary in this movie to inform us that, in Hollywood and every other business, Jews, male and female, disguise their national origin "for professional reasons." Yet the point receives more than adequate emphasis when Peck's conspicuously gentile fiancée cannot persuade him at first that she would marry him if he were *really* Jewish. The plain issue is that of "successful masquerade" —for which the best, and certainly the most lucrative, formula (it sticks out like Peck's manicured thumb) is that of being a Hollywood actor. Significantly, the fate of Garfield, Peck, and wives in their anti-Semitic suburb is never seen; Hollywood knows very well when to draw the curtain.

Crossfire provided a perfectly complemental example of the professional ethic; here a candid-camera Jew is dealt death by an equally candid-camera gentile. Moral: Those who passively and naïvely accept their Jewishness (that is, do nothing to "improve" accent or physiognomy or mannerism) are open to victimization. Once again, the nominal gentile is physically superior to the Jew with whom he is juxtaposed; by this "superiority" is indicated that social eligibility residing in a limited brand of personal attractiveness. For the gentile fascist, the casting department wittily employed an ideal "G.I." physical type if ever there was one, Robert Ryan, who found it as possible to look villainous as Sam Levene, who played the Jew, has found it possible in some villain's role *he* has played in the past. The social eligibility ratio, according to the Hollywood telescoped standard of sex appeal, manners, and looks, is the same in both the movies under discussion; the higher ratio lies, whether he be hero or villain, *with the gentile*.

In these "problem films," we are viewing a "realism" self-consciously equating itself with life, so that our cue is not to think of lack of personability or physical irregularity as a "talent possibility," having an internal side exploitable by comedian or character actor, but only as something to be *compensated for* in society and the extratheatrical business world. Thus, Hollywood, by indirectly elevating gentile above Jew, is "anti-Semitic" only in that its absolutist creed is *pro-assimilative*.

Now, how may this simon-pure creed be stated in broader terms? It is precisely the kind of snobbery operating in "beauty" and "talent" contests everywhere, based on the truly *mass* ideal of good looks and good manners encompassing every element important for any job except the specific technical competence. In other words, Hollywood preëminently stands for the showcase aspect of all business—if, above all, of its own. Its pleas for social tolerance can be only a side dish simply because it is never serious about anybody's business but its own.

Amazingly enough, the Negro films follow suit in being fables of mere illusion despite the indelible sign of black skin which, in two cases, "haunts" the protagonists. Here, too, the human personality is presented as a showcase, reinforcing the implication that, legally white or colored, the human being is to be regarded, as far as possible, as a flexible and a surface phenomenon. The legend of *Gentleman's Agreement* is archetypal because it possesses an automatically reversible logic as though it were two sides of a magician's cloak: A Jew may successfully masquerade as a gentile just as a gentile may successfully masquerade as a Jew. Isn't this the *easiest way* to deal with prejudice? Of course, when it comes to the Negro situation and its known statistics, the shoe must be subjected to a certain compensation mechanism to prevent its pinching too hard (in Hollywood) the other foot of the social problem. The Negro G.I. in *Home of the Brave*, being a pure African type, can never conceivably pass himself off as white. This man's absorption with the color of his skin is so pathological that his dearest wish might be that, some night, the Lord would change his color and modify his features so that, even as Scott Carter of *Lost Boundaries* and Pinky herself (both bred "white" through intermarriage), he too might "pass."

The producers of *Home of the Brave* went to a great deal of trouble to prove that a Negro may have all the characteristics of one of filmdom's leading juveniles except a white skin and the corresponding type of feature. The young Negro here has dignity, natural gentility, and most personable African-ness, suitably exploited by close-ups in which a trembling lip (signifying suppressed emotion) puts him in a histrionic class with Jennifer Jones. Hence, while showing the character thus impersonated as a victim of race prejudice, largely due to his own neurosis, Hollywood sneaks in a good dose of its own cult of personability. Where, however, does "Hollywood talent" land this black hero, Peter Moss? Paradoxically, it doesn't save him from the trauma doubly occasioned by the persecution of a white G.I. and by the gruesome death of his own white G.I. chum. A psychological fault of the film is that this persecution by a G.I. (malcontent with the war because it has displaced him from a well-paying desk job) is shown as a routine, subcultural prejudice against black skin. The truth, according to Moss' personality, is that the white G.I. is irritated specifically by Moss' modest, tacit assumption of social equality as a well-spoken, educated being, a "Hollywood talent" supposedly out of place with a black skin.

However, the Negro's downfall (shown physically by his inability to walk) is duly staged under excruciating circumstances on a Japanese island, and has to be unstaged by the rather melodramatic maneuvers of an omniscient army psychiatrist. Presumably, Moss is enabled to walk again through the destruction of his delusion that a black skin is a fatal curse; thus he is restored to normal life and locomotion by yet another delusion: that some sort of neutral skin color exists in the abstract, indeed, the very "color" that is meant by "equality" on the democratic politico-economic "palette." Since the Hollywood "glamor act" is unachievable in the case of an indelibly black skin, recourse must be taken to the larger and more hazardous "act" of the equality myth. Just how

99

hazardous this is, is cruelly indicated at the end, when a white G.I. amputee offers to become Moss' partner in the restaurant business the Negro wants to start. The moral is made overt through the film's articulate testimony: A white man must lose an arm to equate himself in worldly eligibility with a black man having both arms.

Yet soon after *Home of the Brave* appeared, *Lost Boundaries* arrived to show, in no minced terms, that racial intermarriage is one sure-fire way for the black race, eventually, to stage its "equality act." This is the story of a Negro doctor and his bride, light enough to pass easily for white, whom circumstance effectually tempts into betraying their original decision to live "as Negroes." Unlike *Gentleman's Agreement,* it is an *explicit* tale of successful masquerade by members of an underdog group. Certainly, with its conventionally attractive hero and heroine typifying the millions of technical "Negroes" passing as whites in the United States, *Lost Boundarie*s is quietly aimed at sensationalism and quietly hits its mark.

We have already seen a roster of films in which persons extraordinary and ordinary have been restored to normalcy and/or their regular professions by psychiatric treatment (*The Seventh Veil, Spellbound, The Snake Pit,* and the like). In *Lost Boundaries,* orthodox religion performs a very similar restorative role as a public act; here, a minister's sermon persuades the small-town community which has discovered, with appropriate alarm, that its well-loved doctor and his family are "Negroes" that, since God made us all and this doctor is an incarnate symbol of good deeds, the town should continue to keep him and to behave as if no Negro blood flowed in his veins. The townspeople decide in Dr. Carter's favor.

But what, the question instantly supervenes, has made possible such a ceremony of purification? Not merely the factor that the Carters are absolute models of the conservative middle class (though this too is essential) but most necessarily the a priori factor that they were made eligible for such a socioeconomic success *through racial intermarriage.* Thus, what the white minister fundamentally puts forward in the Carters' behalf *as Negroes* is that their progenitors showed the good intention of *assimilation,* a good intention which Scott Carter and his bride personally have carried out to the last dot. Assimilation is thus placed before the Negro and white public by this movie as a sensational transformation act that has an excellent chance of success without as much trouble as the Carters ran into when their secret leaked out. Hollywood's internal angle is simple—only through the supplementary asset of "good breeding" (speech, deportment, and so on) could the Carters have put across their "act" as whites! To have a white skin is only the beginning; one must learn to live up to it in every way.

In her film, Pinky too is equipped in no mean sense to put across her act in the South as she has done up North, but she is harassed by a "race conscience" into sacrificing the prospective social career of being a white doctor's wife in the North in order to establish and head a nursing clinic for Negro children in her home town. An eccentric old lady whom Pinky tended on her deathbed has left her the means by willing her a fine house and grounds. Worthy of note is that the letter of the law (including especially the "human law" involved in the Hippocratic oath) receives a great deal of tacit respect in these problem pictures about Negroes. In *Pinky,* the process of legal justice, somewhat to one's surprise, triumphs below the Mason-Dixon line as the process of divine justice in *Lost Boundaries* triumphs above it. The southern court decides against the claim of the rascally relatives who contest the old lady's will. The issue of both movies is that of national institutionalism: religious and civil law as nondiscriminating toward race. The hint to Negroes is plain enough: Keep within the law at all costs because it intends to save you as the army psychiatrist saved the black victim of "race trauma" in *Home of the Brave.* As for Pinky, she is certainly no "Red." Her film vehicle backs up democratic institutionalism 100 per cent by means of racist intention and racist result; before the last fade-out, we witness Pinky's clinic in full bloom.

In transcending orthodox religion, while offering no opposition to it, Hollywood is the one "church" whose shibboleths cannot even be remotely construed to interfere with any economic or political law in the United States, or democratic amendment thereto.[1] When the studios have portrayed the Negro as worthy of the smiles of divine and civic justice as well as of the fickle goddess, Fate, the ostensible inference is that Hollywood has contributed its tithe to racial tolerance as one tin cup and to patriotism as another. Does it matter that the racial thesis of *Pinky* in terms of general ethics contradicts that of *Lost Boundaries?* For one thesis does contradict the other. Substantially, *Lost Boundaries* says to the white-skinned Negro: "Pass if you will—and God be with you!" *Pinky* says to him: "Don't pass even if you can—adopt racism: It needs you." This quite unintentional propagandistic *double-entendre* is made possible only by one thing, which is underlined by another visible phenomenon that is coincidental only in the temporal sense.

On the same bill with *Pinky* at its original Broadway run, a newsreel carried the face and Charles Laughtonish voice of an American Federation of Labor official who, just returned from Europe and reporting in behalf of the theatrical professions, said that American movies are having an "impact" on European audiences grown tired of the "propaganda" handed out by Russia and reacting in favor of the American films' "entertainment." The apparent contradiction between this opinion and the social message of *Pinky* and the others, is more complex than the sort to be solved merely by a semantics of rhetoric. It is not that the function of propaganda is also to be entertainment, but that the function of entertainment is also to be propaganda—not only for American democracy, of course, but likewise for that Universal Church of monolithic socio-economic eligibility which is a tangible element of this democracy, and of which Holly-

[1] One may technically remain a Negro, of course, while not looking or behaving like, or pretending to be, one. The law does not require white "Negroes" to declare themselves except for the possible purpose of legal documents.

wood (with its trade unions as well as its stars) is, as I am arguing, the self-conscious shrine.

Does the ideology of one Hollywood product contradict another's? What do you know! The wiseacres of show business—naturally including everyone involved and certain others—are not disturbed; only a "nut" would bring up the point in the first place. If, in *Pinky*, the Hollywood cult casually sacrifices, to the ethical ideal of racism, the rewards automatically open to white-skinned beauty (for example, the chance to win the title of Miss America), there is a bromidic cachet right in the plot to justify it in cardinal terms of "the faith." The film guilds of Hollywood can hardly be wrong on a question like this: In motion pictures, "entertainment" precedes and ultimately defines "propaganda." Our heroine experiences one of those "private failures" combined with a "public success" which is a sentimental cliché of the biographic romances; if she deliberately flops in putting across her private act, she stages her public one with a vengeance, converting a southern ancestral mansion into a black social institution right in the faces of her white tormentors.

All over again, we have the perennial Hollywood underdog's smashing, publicity-getting triumph. One can imagine the solemn "radical" minds of the West Coast congratulating themselves that Pinky voluntarily gives up the kind of glamor that the "pinkies" of real life presumably would choose without hesitation: marriage to a white man and a white future! The "sacrifice," however, is obviously predicated on a richly furnished *power of choice* which, on the whole, should be received as welcome flattery by numerous individuals of the Negro race. With box-office receipts on the downgrade, the sensationalism from the white viewpoint is ideally wedded to a sensationalism from the black viewpoint. It is, as it might be phrased, "the sort of publicity which Negroes couldn't pay to get." Even the Universal Church of Hollywood cannot get along without journalism, and it is elementary journalistic wisdom that, on such a scale, the problem film accomplishes, beyond all speculative "social good," one unquestionable and massive public mission: It super-glamorizes the commonplace act of "passing."

From the serious ethical standpoint, the pith of the matter has not even been touched by Hollywood's innocents, though it is right under their noses. It is nothing but the problem of "identity" of whose "mistaken-ness" they have made such straight-faced sport with Jew and Negro. Long before existentialism, the drama of Oedipus helped to teach us, through art, the importance of personal identity. What is the true problem of identity in *Pinky* and *Lost Boundaries?* Aunt Dicey, Pinky's black grandmother, who can neither read nor write, is a more instinctive metaphysician, one would hazard, than any of the movie's creators. However blindly, she puts her finger on the essence of the matter when she says reproachfully to Pinky: "People shouldn't deny *what they is*." Aunt Dicey's point is that *being* a Negro, Pinky should behave as though she were.

102   But Aunt Dicey, and Hollywood too, should be told that Pinky, as her white skin informs all and sundry, "is" a "Negro" *only because of a legal technicality,* only because white society arbitrarily ordained that she be "black" rather than "white." On the contrary, biology plainly states that she is both, and probably more "white" than "black." Strictly speaking, although the color line is in some regions a social absolute, the mulatto is a *borderline identity.* But Pinky finds the borderline problem insoluble and must cheat 50 per cent of her rights as a human individual by deciding only for the black side. How literal the classic "black or white" choice of moviedom's fiction has become! It was overlooked, dramatically, that Pinky's "white" symbolizes just as much a *group* duty, biologically speaking, as her "black" blood, and in choosing a black social identity, she is convicting her progenitors of the social "crime" of assimilation—she is, in effect, denying the very moral will of fused black and white that brought her into being.

In giving up "personal glamor" for "race glamor," Pinky is the heroine of a curiously paradoxical exploitation of the Hollywood professional myth, whose conditions I have already explained. Objectively, one might quarrel over Pinky's logic as conceivably reactionary in that Negroism perforce militates against tolerance in putting up sexual barriers that hold the races apart. But patently, Hollywood's angle leaps clear of the argument. Behind all the means which white-passing Negroes and potentially gentile-passing Jews have in common for attaining and consolidating their "masquerade" is a simple motto for garden-variety (or Hollywood-conscious) democrats: Every De-Racializing Move is a *Sure* Move in the Direction of Glamor. This axiom, indeed, is uncontradictable on the level of personal charms and personal success so ascendant in an era of individual competitiveness and in a society where the dominant moral ideas derive their ideal nature from the ideal aspect of the economy.

Hollywood, I dare say flatly in conclusion, fulfills the place of a Universal Church in propagating the sacred image of a basically snobbish democracy: an anti-intellectual, "nonsectarian," and socially crass *personability.* Essentially, it is but a hardened vaporization of the old melting pot doctrine on which the economy of the New World is explicitly built. It has been gradually converted to the Hollywood perspective, I should say, because the existing economy structures have been found inadequate to totally unite a democracy retaining (all sentimental optimism to the contrary notwithstanding) serious racial and religious differences.

In placing a quasi-celestial ideal of human appearance and behavior before a democratic public, the melting pot doctrine via Goldwyn and Zanuck veers from its original economic status to a socio-biological status, by whose regulation orthodox religion as a serious force goes underground, and is allowed to speak up for all to hear (as in *Lost Boundaries*) *only* in behalf of the melting-pot doctrine. In this Hollywood ideology, assimilation is a higher stage of tolerance, as $5,000 weekly is a higher stage then $1,000 weekly and as going out with Jeanne Crain is a higher stage than going out with her stand-in. It might be nominally identified as the Cult of the Divine Robot, in which mixing all the racial colors is supposed to produce, not a depressing gray, but a glowing pink, and in which an undesirable religion may be overcome by changing one's nose or taking a course in diction.

104

For Shadows, Against Pull My Daisy

Shadows is *not* part of the Beat da-da-da. Beatism is a wee, wee cult with a public-relations palate as visible as that of the Wolf when he impersonated Little Red Riding Hood's grandmother. *Pull My Daisy*, one of its sugar-capped teeth, focuses on a tendency with its roots in the international avant-gardism of the twenties. The most striking thing about the modern school from which *Pull My Daisy* stems is its lack of historical consciousness in its own field: its obvious debt (incarnate in Jack Kerouac) to a bagful of Dada and pre-Dada, Surrealism, Gertrude Stein, Ernest Hemingway, Scott Fitzgerald, E. E. Cummings, and Henry Miller. The grabbing is as big as the bag. One might even, on heavier thought, add to the above list. Kerouac's personal contribution, the sound-track which is the purely literary facet of *Pull My Daisy*, reeks of the recherché. Oh, Kerouac has a knack! But so has Danny Kaye—it's just a case of different fields. The very fact that the film grew from Kerouac's unproduced play, *The Beat Generation*, and that it became, in many ways, a designing improvisation, points straight to what I mean.

A few professional critics saluted the authenticity of *Pull My Daisy* with familiar quotable clichés. "Fresh," for example. The film's as fresh as a frozen green pea, which of course, in a manner of speaking and after all, is an authentic green pea with a relatively new un-freshness. Pompous acclaim of mere authenticity is one of the great moral and intellectual failings of our time: a time drunk on the sweet fragrance of statistics. Some inconsequential, undesirable, and tainted things are habitually "authentic." Hilter was authentic, and so was Stalin. Concentration camps, like riots and demonstrations, are as authentic as American reform legislation. They're the tit-for-tat known historically as the dialectic. Well, then, everything is in its way authentic, even the atom bomb—with the single exception (if Allen Ginsberg, as quoted by Jacques Barzun, is to be believed) of man himself. Man is "obsolete." In the mouths of men, this puts every authenticity in question, and sure enough, Ginsberg is made to say in *Pull My Daisy:* "Bishop are

105

holy flowers holy?" Aside from questions, the only remaining authenticity is a sort of deaf-mute atavism, problematically blind.

Objectively, it can be insisted, Beatism is a collective form of authenticity. One can't deny its existence or that its existence has a joy of its own. (Yeah, man—to be a bit obsolete.) But "joy"? I'd like to correct the word from my corner. Euphoria, I think, as the antithesis of *angst*. Yet the Beat collective naturally escapes definition. Its pleasure like its pain, its *angst* like its euphoria, show through like the latest juvenile delinquent to be technically embarrassed by the public spotlight. What accounts for this quality? A built-in non self-criticism, defying criticism by anyone or any standards. Grim or gory (by token), carefree, airy, ecstatic, blah or flatfooted, in bad taste or ephemerally inspired, professionalized or "at home," it's to be enjoyed because it "had to be," and if not enjoyable, it's you who don't "belong," not it. *Lebensraum*, at a minimum. That is: Shantih.

If, despite orders from headquarters, the sun of history still shines, it is possible to conclude that the Beat canon is a sort of art-processing derived from thought-smashing. Kerouac's script for *Pull My Daisy* (printed in paperback) ends: "Hello, gang./Da da da da da/And they're going dada da da dada da da. . . . Let's go. 'sgo, 'sgo. . . . Off they go." To interpolate an addendum before the silence: "Ta ta. Goonight. Goonight. Good night, ladies, good night, sweet ladies, good night, good night." To let it settle: "Datta. Dayadhvam. Damyata." I forgot to add T. S. Eliot to the above list. *He* knew where all that stuff came from. Kerouac and his gang aren't aware of Eliot's presence; at least, they're trying to forget it as they try to forget the presence of those others. In any case, other presences (as per Beat) are irrelevant. The world is for the eternally young, etc. etc. etc. One may note that when the Surrealists made automatic texts a method, however, they were *getting away from* Eliotism, not being fed at its breast.

To put in a word for historical consciousness in the arts, no one was more historically conscious than the highly distinguished Alfred Jarry, creator of Ubu. The avant-garde impulse nevertheless began finding history irksome, for reasons best known to itself, and having gone through the wringers of Dada and Surrealism, its free speech has become, at last, less the artist's privilege than the soap-boxer's arrogation. The spotlight of publicity has always been something the Belligerent Bohemian needed like a warm bath: it's quieting (at first, anyway). The film camera, in such cases, is a pretty good substitute for a warm bath. *Pull My Daisy* was meant to document the performances supposedly going on in the tenement-like homes the impoverished Beats have made, statistically, into their Waste Lands. The film is a contemporary version of everything colloquial in Eliot's poem: the poet-witness is set off against the common people and their poverty on grounds where he is, of course, an ambiguously welcome trespasser. The scene witnessed by the camera eye in *Pull My Daisy* is as old as the location of the Provincetown Playhouse. Never before today has bohemian revolt been considered so ofay—and never before, consistently, has the outcast tramp-poet been so much a theatrical charade. *Pull My Daisy* is an audio-visual paean to this fact. I don't think *this* authenticity can be denied. Yet by an obscure act of will, the Beats *have* cut off historic consciousness. None of them is quite so anonymous as the late, unlamented John Rose Gildea, and none of them—unless I am far, far wrong —will end up like Maxwell Bodenheim.

To me, the look of the pressure on literature and its history which has made the Beat fission possible is, whether on page or film-reel, a flotsam of literary tags unstably imbedded in an indescribable jelly of content. Sassy youth, moral anarchism, cadged wine and beer (see soundtrack) are as much window-dressing as anything else. Specific literary effort sometimes rises above them. The best contribution to the paperback text of the film is not in the film itself. This is the amusingly pornographic song of the same title by Kerouac and Ginsberg; though rather static, it has a real literary imagination. With one line sourly bowdlerized, an actress sings two partial stanzas in the film. The way Hollywood-type censorship creeps in here is like the odor of the casting-office that connects the dramatis personae of *Pull My Daisy* with the dramatis personae of Shaw's Salvation Army play. Compassing the world of the "Salvation Army," the Frank-Leslie-Kerouac film has the same holier-than-thou cynicism. Aren't the Beats the "Salvation Army" of the avant-garde? Damyata, ineffably. Somehow, too, the film's persons seem to have been filtered into the vicinity of contemporary Tenth Street through Arthur Millerism or latterday Clifford Odetism.

I believe that no grain of such affiliations (quite innocent, of course, for everything Beat is innocent) adheres to *Shadows*, so that any mentioned connection between the two films seems unfortunate and inauthentic. If they can be classed together, it is only on the loosest level of current film conventions. In fact, the shots in *Pull My Daisy* are more self-consciously "art photography" than anything in *Shadows*. This loosest level, I suppose, may soon get to be called the Flow of Life Film, something making that notable flow more comme-ci, comme-ça, than does the Nouvelle Vague, which, to be readily marketable, had to make raw sex and other popular conventions a part of the flow. Surely, some foreign directorial talent has mined poetry from this very flow, and *erotic* poetry, but the comparative value of such achievements is eminently arguable. Let that point, however, pass.

Shadows has been surprisingly well appreciated while mostly for the wrong reasons. One wrong reason is its superficial technical kinship with *Pull My Daisy* and the Documentary Film. No one, I believe, except the author of an article on Cassavetes in a small West Coast film magazine, has noticed the relation between the method of *Shadows* to that of Chekhov in his plays and especially his short stories. *Shadows* approaches its subject with the same casual directness as Chekhov his subjects; it punctures life, as it were, the skin of life, and as the bleeding goes on, vanishes before the outflow is stanched. The American literary tradition echoing Chekhov is Sherwood **107**

Anderson more than Hemingway, and that very talented short-story writer, Eudora Welty. This is the basic *style* that Cassavetes instinctively followed. It takes a few characters and reveals their life-situation; the situation moves behind the veil of full consciousness and yet it communicates. Orson Welles and Jean Renoir are among the very few commercial directors of note who have used techniques homogenizing plot, character, social scene and ordinary talk into one unified, if baroque and only partly intelligible, surface. The relation of this effect to the way dialogue is employed in *The Waste Land* is close. Life is a surface which, from this viewpoint, is tantalizingly inarticulate, laced with enigmas of sound and sight, fleetingly submerged in its own volubility, retreating (when least expected) into symbolic idioms.

This stylistic trait is clearly related to modern ambiguity in the arts. Meaning lies behind meaning, consciousness within consciousness. You have to catch their contact on the move. Everything in *Pull My Daisy* steers willynilly toward the self-consciously literary, at times the arty. Without pause its gab unwinds from the reel created by this much practised self-consciousness. The characters in *Shadows* are not puppets of such literary lazy-daisiness, trademarked by every artistic movement in the first half of the century. However, *Shadows* does suffer from the Village tradition of sitting around and bee-essing (I follow the bowdlerizing trend) as a form of passive, futile protest against having nothing else to do; thus when something *is* done, it may well be catastrophic. In *Shadows*, the passage taking place in the garden of the Museum of Modern Art should be clipped from the film; it's bloodcurdlingly gauche and irrelevant to the theme. I fancy it's masochistic, perhaps some penance imposed by Cassavetes on himself, or else his sadistic exploitation of the masochism he found emerging from the film's fringe-of-culture milieu: highbrow chatter forces its way to the surface of a party scene and "modern art" reproductions stare disconcertingly from casually encountered walls.

All *that* belongs to the naiveté of the milieu Cassavetes is portraying; it is not the meat of the matter. The *meat* is solely the meaning inherent, and poignantly inherent, in human relationships. I believe these relationships have been discussed by reviewers only on a superficial plane because, in a day of racial integration, the theme is a very tender one. That this "tenderness" has its own ambiguity is part of *Shadows'* accomplishment. The dark, African-type big brother, mothering, fathering and otherwise coddling his white-looking younger half-brother and half-sister, is martyred not by their dependence on him, but by their urgent temptation to find love and fulfillment by passing for white. This may be a delusion on their part, a delusion of youth, of inexperience, even of a lack of intelligence; it becomes real, nevertheless. If the younger brother's climactic reaction against the "color" atmosphere of the party in his home is basically an incestuous emotion he has for his sister (which is a possible motivation), the indisputable truth is that in effect it is a protest—however transitory, however unconscious—against the Negroid itself. This is a daringly candid element of Cassavetes' story. Ostensibly he developed the action with his actors' help; they themselves felt, or had empathy for, the feelings of the fictional persons. The three leading roles are first-rate performances by any standard, on Broadway or off, and have the best virtues of so-called Method acting. The crowded scene where the big brother (a jazz musician) is discussing business with his agent, while simultaneously his brother tries to get some money out of him, is a miracle of polyphonic, polyvisual style.

The crisis is precipitated when the young girl goes to bed with a young white man. It is the most natural sort of sexual incident in the world. They fall hard and the affair immediately looks serious. Almost at once, then, he discovers her Negroid strain when her dark half-brother surprises them in her apartment. Instinctively revolted, the white man shows it, and is ordered to leave the house by the girl's big brother. She morally sides with her dark brother, accepting as fatal her allegiance to his race and personal gratitude to him. Bolstered by a certain moral horror of her lover's race-prejudice, her gratitude seems the deciding factor. But obviously she is shattered, her future looms empty; she feels a prisoner in a debt of blood and honor casting a shadow over her life. The play between skin-color and mood in the action and the film's title is another of its scanted merits. One feels, as everything drifts into stalemate, that inside the three people a perfectly private agony is growing—an agony that shows its stripe when the younger brother strikes a black girl who makes up to him at a party given at his home, is roughed by his big brother, and rushes out.

Told in its offhanded, somewhat deceptive way, *Shadows* could have been the opposite of delicate. But Cassavetes had a saving intelligence for what he was doing. He possesses a film sense and human tactfulness, a feeling for the inner person's dignity and the facts encompassing it. So many would like to have this quality today, and it's often imputed with insufficient evidence. Yet I know of no film but *Shadows* which offers it in so precise and ample, so truly considered, a form. It is much superior to any other film I know with a common racial dilemma for its major theme. As a jazz musician, the black big brother is far from brilliant; this fact alone is an inspired touch of candor: he has only creature-kindness to offer for admiration. Whatever personal "talents" may lie in the younger brother and sister seem to have been muffled by racial and personal allegiance, fostered to some extent by their economic dependence on their brother. All this is brought to the breaking point by the girl's love affair. She has always known she could "pass" but she keeps to a mixed society, being drawn away from it on an occasion when a boy friend takes her to the party where she meets her lover-to-be. After the scene where her lover is shown the door, there remains only the painful birth of the whole situation's insolubility. True to their big brother, each passing black, or at least "neutral" while looking white, neither girl nor boy feels free. New tenderness for the girl is awakened in her big brother after her dis-

109

astrous affair; without admitting it to himself, he begins to divine the rock-bottom plight of her feelings. She longs to pass for white, to leave the marginal world where her big brother must stay. Does she have incestuous feelings for her white-looking brother? Perhaps. Probably he does for her. At any rate, it seems as much his sympathy for her, as awareness that his dilemma is like hers, that causes his wild outbreak and his fight with his brother.

And where does he work off his shame—his shame at feeling revolt against part of his blood, at striking the Negress, at his inability to solve his dilemma? In brute action, of course, in the gang action when he and his "white" buddies flirt with some other fellows' girls and get beaten up in an alley. If we decide that this is, in one respect, his "black" masochism, I don't think the conclusion is offensive; it is simply true, and *Shadows* is its medium. It may not be final, this masochism. At the very end, the boy splits from his friends to let his agony purge or despoil him in isolation. Is he really alone? This is part of the Chekhovian suspense-ending.

Shadows is subtle—and everything could have been expected of it but subtlety! Why not subtlety? The point has nothing to do with the film's style or its subject-matter. The appearance of a film-maker of power and insight, one with this fresh and difficult sense of style, and the courage to reveal human depths raw with controversy, was, on the face of things, highly improbable. Perhaps *Shadows* could be better edited. I don't even know if I saw the "better" version of it. But such questions are here the nuances of artistic virtue. Cassavetes had his insight, his inspired theme, and made them work together with his actors and his medium . . . To let the material speak for itself! To show life "as it is"! Never to impose artificial, shopworn patterns on human behavior! All these ideal goals are claimed for the documentary school of film-making. They are all very well, and yet, as hundreds of films attest, they can at times produce hollow shells, pretentious banalities, an arbitrary flattening of the life-dimension, a perverse shunning of all depth of feeling and idea.

I'm afraid that the Documentarists and the Flow-of-Lifers may consider my attribution of subtlety to Cassavetes' film (especially as I construe its meaning) as some sort of smear, something for him, and the supposed tendency represented by his film, to repudiate. However that may be, I am glad I could present my argument in this particular form in this particular place. My desire—wistful as it must be—was to demonstrate that a presumed art-style film, *Pull My Daisy*, placed next to a presumed documentary-style film, *Shadows*, can reverse these classifications; the former's pretensions are futile and unfresh, far removed from life's center, the latter's achievement is misunderstood, fresher and more important than anyone seems to have felt, and close to life's center. And I think that time (if it's any good any more) will prove this.

To the above, I can add my genuine surprise that Cassavetes' film made for Paramount, *Too Late Blues*, sustains nearly all the original and interest-

110

ing qualities of *Shadows*, even if we see them, as it were, in the disguise of certain commercial formulas. This disguise betrays itself in the fact that here, unlike *Shadows*, the actors do not invariably get contact with Cassavetes' intentions, whether because of the studio shooting-schedule or their individual resistance, I am not in a position to know. Discounting the lesser co-operation by the actors (observable most in Stella Stevens, who is still brilliant in spots), *Too Late Blues* remains earmarked as a Cassavetes work, worthy of the most earnest attention. I should say altogether that Cassavetes remains the only individual now preoccupied with big films who strictly confines himself to being an expert in *human* rather than *public* relations. This goes for the flashy new crop of foreign directors with very, very few exceptions.

The "popular" elements witnessed in *Shadows* are likewise in *Too Late Blues:* unblunted (here very promiscuous) sex; a whopping scene of brute violence; the exact realism of the complex surface offered by life as it is lived: the cross currents of talk and behavior as well as the ambiguity of moral currents, the timidity and plotting of people puzzled by themselves and shy of outright commitment. However, one of the surprising things in *Too Late Blues*, which is the partial odyssey of a jazz-band leader and composer with delusions of grandeur, is how much people *do* come out in the open when the fat is in the fire of interpersonal relations. I am sure all the film's scenes were deliberately, professionally rehearsed, yet many have the effect of using hidden cameras and hidden microphones—so cannily, so uncompromisingly does Cassavetes get his grip on his material. Perhaps he exaggerates! Most interesting artists in the world have "exaggerated." I still maintain that such extravagance is based on the most intelligent observation of human beings to air itself these days in film studios.

Critically speaking, I should wish *not* to seem to exaggerate. But placed against the film's demerits, its virtues, I think, shine out irresistibly. For once, the saturating light of bold studio photography is justified by the force of what is being seen and heard; it is vulgar, it is stupid, it is often corny— just like the characters themselves. Yet Cassavetes has that subtle detachment from the nature of his material that defines the truthfulness of art as distinguished from the quasi-truthfulness of mere reporting or comic-strip populism. When he makes the hero (played with inspiration by none other than Bobby Darin) balmy with love, obsessively self-starred, maddened, corruptible, cowardly, cynical, brutal, and brutally sentimental, it seems not "for effect" but from respect for the human facts. In all his characters—including the band leader's vindictive, incredibly hard-shelled agent—we see head-on (in pitiless, breathtaking close-ups of faces and speeches) the automatic reflexes of daily, hourly emotions. "This is my view of life, my view of myself," each individual bursts out, "take it or leave it!—meaning *me!*" Human beings slip from kindliness and romantic softness into unconcealed anger, cruelty, and cynicism, without realizing, apparently, that transitions are taking place. This is a sizeable contribution to naturalizing the film's imaginative view of

111

contemporary life. Will Hollywood annihilate this extraordinary talent?—
that is, will Cassavetes *let* it be annihilated?

The Cult

The great cult of the average movie-goer is a curious mixture, containing, among other things, the lay religions of snobbery and social climbing. These have oddly masqueraded, in social-problem pictures of recent years, as the "evils" of racial and religious prejudice. The true content of such films has been the potent glamor of the industry's own profession, one element of which (as signalized in this study of profiles) is a desirable type of nose. Here, light ironically sets off two "opposed" physiognomies having but a single aim: all those privileges, both professional and unprofessional, to be won by conformance with a given personality norm.

Crossfire

Courtesy RKO Radio Picture.

Les Liaisons Dangereuses (Vadim)

Sweet and Sour (Baratier)

Nowadays, for art or anti-art, the camera eye is inch by inch denuding the human body and its private life; opposite are scenes from two films of the past decade that illustrate how daring a public inquisitor the camera has become: the eye on the wall symbolically eavesdrops on ordinary fornication, while (ostensibly in a satire on Cinéma Vérité) a young camera fiend lassoes her boyfriend to induce him to confess his neurosis to her and the world, too. The still below, at first sight, may look like a deliberately unguarded moment from a bona fide Happening; actually, it is symptomatic of a remarkably controlled, remarkably pointed spontaneity. Yet far too often, in the mid-sixties, Happening-like films from the Underground exploit wild, crudely planned shindigs only from childish exhibitionism and the impudent disregard for form and meaning.

Shadows (Cassavetes)

This and the two succeeding pages contain examples of the cult of the human image as reflected in the artistic revision which it endured from the end of the last century when, even in sculpture, it took on the melting lines of something vaporous and illusive, to its recent total immersion in abstract space. These versions of it should be contrasted with the way its identity, on previous pages, is preserved even while accorded an illusory and dreamlike aspect by cinematic devices. From Rodin's classical vestige, the human image proceeded in painting to the neo-African fetish (Brancusi) and parody by the studio armature (de Chirico), through identification with manufactured objects such as furniture, machines, and clothes (Léger and Duchamp), to extreme hieroglyphic (Miró) and on to visual punning with all nature (Tchelitchew), culminating in an ingenious "costume" of spatial planes (Marca-Relli).

Rodin: *Orpheus and Eurydice*
Courtesy The Metropolitan Museum of Art

de Chirico: *Troubadour*
Courtesy The Museum of Modern Art

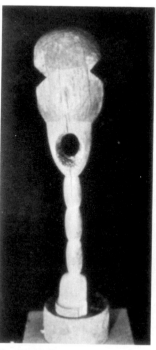

Brancusi: *Socrates*
Courtesy The Museum of Modern Art

Miro: *Group of Women* (detail
Courtesy Mrs. Marcel Duchamp

Duchamp: *La Marié mis à nu, par ses célibataires, même*
Courtesy Philadelphia Museum of Art

Léger: *Le Grand Déjeuner*   Courtesy The Museum of Modern Art

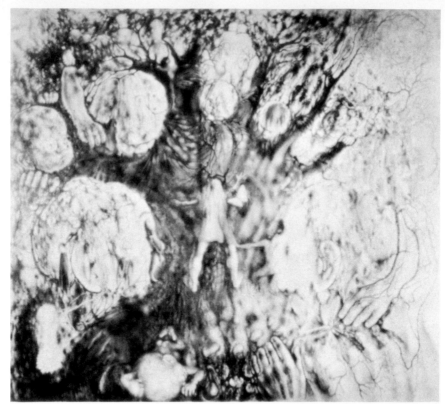

Tchelitchew: *Hide and Seek*

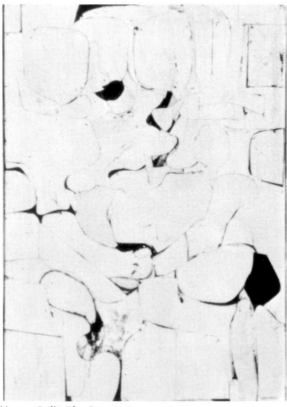

Marca-Relli: *The Strategist*

These two film scenes convey the presence of surcharged human situations of which the film and the stage remain the only adequate media of expression. The memorable Polish film below is probably the most powerful of all movies involving the operation of psychic forces. In the scene from *Ivan the Terrible,* three period-styles, portrayed by human faces, serve a complex development of the dramatic action: the young henchman at the left transmits the smile of an archaic Greek statue to the tyrant Ivan, who is cast in Byzantine features, while the foolish, epicene, but bold physiognomy of the mock emperor stamps him as the "photogenic type" of our film-making century.

Ivan the Terrible (Eisenstein)   *Courtesy Janus Films*

The Dybbuk

Narcissus (Willard Maas-Ben Moore)

The direct imaging of the human face, regardless of style accents or plastic form, possesses an induplicable appeal. The surviving cult of the classic human image seems to depend solely on the movies, whose camera remains the only medium properly equipped (and still willing) to portray its true personality.

The Red and the Black

The Atomic Age at
New York's First Film Festival

Despite the democratic psychology and democratic institutions of our time, our current era is far more oriented to authoritarianism in many spheres than is usually conceded. Besides mass regimentation, there is class regimentation: the process of organizing clique feelings into prevalent high fashion on a large and commercially rewarding scale. With the movies, it is not only that more and more art and revival theatres have sprung up in great metropolitan areas during the past two decades, but that the film archives of art institutions have held more and more ample programs while film festivals in the United States have multiplied so fast it has been hard to keep count of them. For sixteen years, Cinema 16, the New York City film society, spearheaded with its seasonal programs exactly the sort of thing (rarities no longer) that one got in a continuous, indigestible banquet at the First New York Film Festival, 1963, held at Philharmonic Hall.

Since then, the event has become an institution but at that fairly removed moment it was an eye-opener for those who had, indeed, watched the growth of highbrowism in the films from a skeptical distance. As I noted at the time, the space around the box-office at Philharmonic Hall was as populous as a layman's image of far space grown habitable by man. The avant-garde was given a massive push and from all directions; one felt as if the obscurantism of surrealist films, for example, had all along been a false myth foisted on an innocent public; that sick jokes, in-jokes, and the emergent Pop Art had hidden their lucid arclights under a bushel of little experimental films. The latter were not so unprofessional after all, and even if they were, they provided welcome relief from the routinized professional products.

Unquestionably, fashions nowadays are too swift to let us assess them before they fade and are insidiously replaced by fresher novelties. The First New York Film Festival, for instance, displayed a work by a wildcat French aesthete named Jacques Baratier, *Sweet and Sour*; but another Jacques, surnamed Rivette, had already sounded a note just as wild, but more serious, in a film first presented fleetingly by Cinema 16, *Paris Is Ours. Sweet and*

113

Sour was echoed by such wacky commercial exhibits as *What's New Pussycat?* and *The Knack* although both the latter, significantly, had more plot. The impressive thing is the way the films at Philharmonic Hall, in that pristine Festival, sounded in concert a definite psychic vibration, flashing its facets through a kind of vague hysteria.

Dark forces indeed have been and are at work, every hour it seems; tabloid headlines state them literally in jolting scraps; highbrow weeklies essay to discover their omens, anatomy, and destiny; the professional arts stoutly reflect and inflect them. They even inspire promotional conspiracies. These are rather easy to detect since being loud and obvious is their business. Certain conspiracies of nature and man, lying much deeper, have to be worked out in extensive, sometimes cryptic and usually controversial prose by intellectuals in novels and moral commentaries.

On the other hand, the movies are noted and notorious for making such activity look simple—simpler than it is. Hence the movies (it's still true despite all the avant-garde earnestness in the world) are ideal laboratories for publicly negotiable simplifications. Snobs never want to work at mental exercises; thus the snobs of culture appreciate the slightest gestures toward making aesthetic pleasure look simpler, easier, and younger than it is or should be. This is one reason why the Second and Third New York Film Festivals added nothing tangible to that first stunning self-annunciation.

Part of the trick of being a member of the cultural élite (the crème de la crème have grasped this) is to regard the artist's sly thrusts at society as a benign sort of sadism accepted with a grace of masochism to match it. Salvador Dali said of *Le Chien Andalou*, the first film he made with Luis Buñuel, that it would be plunged "right into the heart of witty, elegant and intellectualized Paris with all the weight of an Iberian dagger." Mere film fans have to be informed that this was simply an aspect of the in-culture game. Parisian society had already been initiated into Dadaism and Surrealism and knew the works of de Sade by atavism, if not by heart. Yet a minority of even the creamiest élite has to be shockable (or pretend to be) because that's part of the fun. The élite game in this century has always been to break down more and more barriers of good taste. Nowadays everybody who is anybody likes to believe that Good Taste has been beaten back to its last citadel and given up the ghost—and that this incident has been applauded by everybody who is anybody, for this distinguished person has been on the spot.

When Cocteau showed his *Blood of a Poet* (along with Buñuel's *L'Age d'Or*) at the Vieux Colombier Theatre in Paris, 1931, he compelled the intellectual élite to applaud his Poet's blood-sacrifice: a suicide. As I have written elsewhere, however, the Vicomte de Noailles, who had financed both *L'Age d'Or* and *The Blood of a Poet*, had not allowed Cocteau to use shots in which himself and his friends sat in a box literally applauding the Poet's death as if it were a dramatic spectacle. There were no titled hold-outs either among the spectators at Philharmonic Hall or those who produced or sponsored

114

the films. At the Festival, the history of the avant-garde had all the signs of being homogenized into outbreaks of crowd hysteria in the ritual form of boos, hisses, and applause—in other words, positive collective demonstrations, pro or con. Personally, I noticed a sort of profundity of paradox on the screen as well as in the audience at Philharmonic Hall on this historic occasion. One of the most popular paradoxes of our time may be dubbed "Being Alone Together." Many of the film's fables and fancies, and even some of its modest fictions, reflect the inherent paranoid state of group and interpersonal relationships so that the existent sum of such phenomena may account for the mixed and immodest impact on the audience.

Sweet and Sour is a foolhardy spreading effort to hoke up some fun at the expense of the recently budded Cinéma Vérité school, whose documentary realist method is governed by the man armed with camera and microphone who intercepts citizens going about their business to surprise their thoughts on themselves and great issues of the moment. The walkie-talkie is carried, as it were, into the inner sanctums of Everybody in all his public "nudity." The film makes much of a voyeuristic invasion of privacy, including the pursuit of prostitutes tranquilly plying their trade, by both Vérité interviewers (seen also pursued *by* prostitutes) and the police department actuated by squad car radio. What theme could be more universally dexamil-ish? And it rings with Marshall McLuhan's visionary image of man hemmed in by "electronic circuitry."

My own emphatic impression was that the world's mania for wide and instantaneous communication, visual and verbal, has been converted in our age's paranoid atmosphere into a phobia, and that the synthetic result (well audited by these Festival films) might go by the name of phobio-mania. *Self-exhibition* may be the dominant collective push. As an art-film motif, phobio-mania seems to be replacing sado-masochism through parasitic growth. While the true tradition of the avant-garde is aesthetic-sexual and consciously explored (Baudelaire and successors), emergent phobio mania is morally compulsive and subconsciously explored. It yearns, piously, for the boon of tranquillizers and the false-face of stimulants. *Chemical* circuitry is just as important as *electronic* circuitry.

Hidden sado-masochism and its retroactive fusions, of course, exist and are duly reported by the films. Alain Resnais might be thought the last of art-film directors to give a harsh inflection to the present theme, but that is just what he did with his Festival film, *Muriel*. Set in a French seaport, it deals with tangible, contemporary, commonplace reality, being as labyrinthine as, though far less seductive than, the translucently mannered *Last Year at Marienbad*, to which it seems an antidote. The only fantastic moments of *Muriel* come when the young male lead, back from army service in Algeria, tells in brutally pointblank words how he witnessed the rape, torture, and killing of an Arab girl by soldiers of his platoon; meanwhile he is seated before a TV screen with the old man to whom he makes this spontaneous

115

confession and what we see, as he talks, is only the action on TV: apparently a home-movie record by some French soldier about his comrades innocently lolling and horsing around in Algeria.

Besides the interestingly symptomatic novelties, flatly routine, muscle-proud works also took up space, but these, living in an all-too-familiar vacuum, have no connection with the present thoughts. The psychic vibration made by the word, connection, suggests a much stronger American film than either of the two seen at the Festival: Shirley Clarke's version of Jack Gelber's play, *The Connection*. The hypodermic needle, a transmission agent having various effects, is among the modern symbols of ambivalence—much the same ambivalence that was illustrated with more conscious art in *Le Chien Andalou* by the razor that bang off the first few frames slits a passive woman's eye. This image was, among other things, an epigraph for the whole film's optical assault. Hypodermic needle and razor blade serve benign and malign functions. In the case of drug addicts, whose excruciating ordeal is the subject of *The Connection*, the needle's ambivalent work predicates assorted sado-masochistic incidents.

A particular and parallel, though different, use of the hypodermic is made in an arresting Festival short, *The Jetty*, by Chris Marker. This carries us into future time. Like previous films, this one projected on the Festival screen conditions on earth after an all-out atomic war. Marker's film is notable for its brilliant economy and a poetic psychological depth, showing how much can be accomplished with limited technical means and scope. As man lives miserably underground, scientists among the human survivors predict the race's rapid extinction. To free people, then, from this dire awareness, to escape (as the film puts it) from *time*, experiments with drug-injection are begun in order to give the subject—if he does not die of them—illusions of eternal life either in past or future, whichever he chooses. The hallucinations of the hero, who is repeatedly and successfully injected, form most of the story. A remarkably apt tension issues from the film technique: single frames, quite frozen, seem highpoints of a film from which this succession of stills has been selected. The echo of the film's first primitive experiments to attain motion has a weird eloquence.

One may note that the good-bad function of a drug in *The Jetty* (even its success entails later suffering) is the same function as that in *The Connection*: no futurist fantasy but verifiable reality today. Something else interesting, another modern myth symbol (I almost said status symbol!) exists in *The Connection*, betokening a move from chemical to visual "circuitry." It is the film camera, which as a sometimes hand-held appendage becomes an anthropomorphic member of the cast. The action is a film of a film's being made. While watching *Sweet and Sour*, the riotous walkie-talkie splurge, I recalled moments of *The Connection* when the agonized addicts, waiting for the drug, protest against the film's being made and get tough with its director; that the confused, exhausted director is himself induced to join the pleasure later is part of the sado-masochistic substructure. The sequence in the other film

116

that suggests these addicts' irritability with being filmed concerns a teen-age Cinéma Vérité trainee who lassoes her boyfriend, also a trainee, with a neck microphone and bullies him into "performing." Though he wails like a rock-'n-roller, tears streaming down his face, he goes ahead to confess, rather redundantly, an infancy trauma. The normal impulse toward *privacy* and the pathological impulse toward *withdrawal* are put in crisis by the communication madness. Sex, psychoanalysis, a communication mechanism, all are involved in both the films; they are also involved, with bold sado-masochistic markings, in the *Muriel* episode described above.

On the comic side, a harmless, mildly amusing conception of the film camera as memory-book and welcome-unwelcome invasion of privacy appears in Roberto Rossellini's contribution to the four-part Festival film from Italy and France, *Rogopag*. This recounts the adventure of a pretty airline hostess who is fetichistically, and rather narcissistically, attached to her 8-MM camera; she carries it about with her chiefly, it seems, so that her fiancé in Italy may be kept in touch with her movements by film-letters. Certain moral functions fulfilled by the film-letters turn the camera into another good-bad inquisitorial eye. One might conclude a new form of the All-Seeing Eye of God (an ancient emblem) were among us. The curious anthropomorphic guise arrogated by the camera, its methods of becoming fetich and/or weapon, inquisitor and/or angel of deliverance (read "delivery") align it with all weapon-fetich eyes. It may seem perfectly casual but the truth was that Robert Bresson's disappointing Festival film, *The Trial of Joan of Arc*, plays on the terms of Joan's suspected intimacy with God's wishes by showing her through the peephole used by her priestly enemies to spy on her.

Like shadowing detectives or would-be stranglers and rapists (recall the long film tradition of these), the camera lurks and looms in the labyrinths and on the highways of our paranoid age with a curious intensity, breaking out everywhere as an iconographic signpost. It seems only natural that the eavesdropping faculty of the old *camera obscura* should have had so much revival, especially in avant-garde films for which the keyhole visions of the hero in *The Blood of a Poet* pointed the way long ago. The *filmed* world is both prophetic and retrospective in its imaginable viewpoints and was visualized as such by Elie Faure, the early aesthete of cinematic possibilities. Faure had the Vérité twist. The film camera, he said, might be conceived as penetrating into the past and into the future; even, he specified, back to the events of Jesus' life. However much by chance, more than one Festival film built itself, playfully or seriously, on the same technical assumption.

The Italian Pasolini chose for his part in *Rogopag* an episode about the making of a movie (his own as we learned later) on the life of Christ, in which a Descent from the Cross is being shot in chromo-like color as a sort of *tableau vivant*. Pasolini's satiric mood is boisterous, roguish, and rather reckless in what might be construed as making fun of long-outdated religious reverence in the movies. Yet modern photography suggests the realism of Renaissance master painters as well as Dali's religious themes and **117** their startlingly photogenic nudes. One assumed that the Festival audience responded the more to this episode of *Rogopag* since news of its banning in Italy had arrived at Philharmonic Hall. Not only were conventionally sacred things being profaned and flouted here but also that peripheral "sacredness" of the Customs Authority, which Festival films are officially allowed to escape. The "serious" film on which Pasolini was engaged while he made this brief spoof turned out to be *The Gospel According to St. Matthew*, whose object is to make biblical history look like the ragged documentary manner of Italian films in the forties.

More recent exhibits from Italy (outside the New York Festivals) have kept alive the fantasy mechanisms in modern sensibility. Fellini's *8½* (discussed elsewhere here) is, besides being a delirium of filmic fantasy, an autobiographic document. The confusions of love seem the director-hero's unsettling factor. If we pause to ponder certain symbols, we can note under what odd chameleon forms a thing like Cupid's Arrow can appear: one need only mention (the Festival screen gave testimony) the phallic role of that same devious dart and its fluid ambivalence as a weapon in sado-masochistic emblemology; for example, Baudelaire's little fable: *Mademoiselle Lancet*. The heart of the matter was opened at the Festival in two cases; a switch-blade flashed out in *Knife in the Water*, a smartly done Polish film, and in Jean-Luc Godard's part in *Rogopag* a hunting knife made repeated and highly weighted appearances in strange places. Not at all by coincidence, the setting for the latter is a radioactive Paris of the future, when atomic explosions take place regularly in high altitudes over the city and Parisians seek to counteract the fallout by swallowing huge daily rations of pills.

The story point is that the hero, through whom we hear it all, seems exempt from radioactivity and so, presumably, is reliable as a Vérité reporter. What most affects him about the state of things is that his mistress, a charming zombiesque blonde, starts having odd mental lapses, the most alarming of which is that, when the worried man asks her if she still loves him, she replies smoothly, "I ex-love you." He hasn't misheard, nor have we misheard or misread, for she is induced to repeat her answer. And this is not the most sinister omen about her. The worst is the hunting knife she casually starts wearing. At a public swimming pool, for instance, it is seen thrust conspicuously between her hip and her bikini. At home, as she gets into bed with the narrator, it has just as neat and conspicuous a place in her panties. The film ends in suspense—but not so the new fashion. Godard made his point more explicit in a subsequent Festival year when the ritual of a future society is to have gangs of swimming pool naiads (in *Alphaville*) knife to death lone, defenseless male victims.

I have always liked to think the avant-garde essentially hot-blooded, with a genuine and inspired (even if "morbid") eroticism; however, I fear that lately the avant-garde has helped the art film develop the Cold Nude, which is to say, in essence, the cold-blooded nude of robot-like love-hate. As a concept, this squares out nicely with the phobio-maniac, claustro-agoraphobiac elements of our day's (and this Festival's) wide-angled paranoia. The She or He, thus modishly cold or at least *cool*, would be a plausible figment of drug-induced daydream, whether in *The Jetty* or *The Connection*. One must remember the isolation factor of so much erotic fantasy and that the communication-drive involved is voyeurism and exhibitionism. Some minor, ambiguously amusing data of this trend, the Cold Nude, can be picked up from a half dozen brief animated cut-out films that are post-Dada and pre-Pop in their gay dissection-room manner. I refer to work, familiar to Cinema 16 and other film society audiences, by the Americans Stan Vanderbeek, Robert Preston, and Bruce Conner. The last-named struck a new note with super-speed motion, so that the friction, one might say, produces a "cool" heat.

Amos Vogel, the New York Film Festival's coordinator and former director of the film society, Cinema 16, told me that some six offbeat short films of late years utilize the famous mushroom cloud of the atomic explosion as a sensational climax. Atomic heat, as an idea, makes the blood freeze. As the explosion is used by said films, it may seem a desperately incoherent effort to counteract the black magic in atomic energy with white. As such, it is a symptom of paranoid hysteria, and the more aesthetically clumsy the device appears, the more hysterical (supposedly) the invited laughter. Theoretically, the idea of embarrassing the laughing faculty aims at a salutary moral effect. One scents the aura of our age's bloated *absurdism*. The atomic cloud, per se, has great formal beauty which is only heightened by the moving photograph. Its image, accordingly, is bound to embarrass those who have failed to assimilate the ABC's of sado-masochism or any other vital equation in ambivalent sensations. Laughter, let us reflect, is a classic device for releasing the tension of embarrassment caused by ignorance, uncertainty, and suspense. But laughter as such does nothing to illuminate the terrain hidden behind the device causing it; rather, it serves to obscure that terrain.

By far the two best films at the 1963 Festival, *The Exterminating Angel* and *Harakiri*, were the most terrifying as well as the most tender. Their superlativeness is due entirely to their stature as responsible human documents. The Musem of Modern Art, participating in the Festival with a week of programing hitherto unseen films, usefully displayed a fine work of which the regular exhibitors have been afraid: Kurosawa's *I Live in Fear*. It is a beautifully plotted story about one man's obsessive desire to escape a future atomic war. *Harakiri*, with a subject matter just as violent, is, as the title suggests, cast in an entirely historic mold. It is sumptuously moving, pure enough to be universal, and has nothing to do with modernity as current fashion. Not so *The Exterminating Angel*, made today and *for* today by that talented but besmirched veteran of the avant-garde, Luis Buñuel. I would pardon this film-maker his lifelong concessions to unholy commercialism.

His film is set and was made in Madrid. A party of well-heeled society people, finding they cannot for some entirely mysterious reason leave the **119**

Music Room of the mansion where they have gathered, are caught in a dilemma which does not look at all faked. And not faked either (allowing for some dubious details of execution) is the involuntary collective mood that continues to make them feel consigned to the room as if it were a concentration camp. All the house servants but a butler, who has somehow joined them, have fled the premises earlier, and no help comes from outside as the nightmarish hours go by. So successful is the preternatural atmosphere that one takes for granted the "magical" intervention of some live lambs (presumably held in the kitchen for slaughter) which trot into the Music Room when its occupants are frantic with hunger, get their throats promptly slit, and are roasted. The not-unprecedented allusion to an allegorical or supernatural situation that reproduces a primordial racial experience can be easily grasped.

As one might expect from the same director's *Viridiana*, Buñuel's story is designed to be a deeply satiric-ironic indictment of the decline of religious sensibility and the absence of anything (except, limitedly, all-sensitized art) to replace it. "Being Alone Together" is italicized by the retirement of one romantic couple into a closet to have sex and commit suicide. The great Love Death is made ignoble by the tight environment and the compromised privacy. An especially caustic touch is one lady's effort toward solving the *impasse* by conjuring with some chicken's claws she has brought in her purse "just in case." The siege by the unknown and invisible is lifted when a young woman, inspired by her sexual defloration, suggests they all reconstitute the order of the evening prior to the moment when all realized the room held them captive.

I got the idea that this might mean human society's perpetual review of history in order to determine historical cause, but if so, Buñuel has meshed this too with his paradoxical and eerie structure. The "magic" of recall breaks, we see, the long agonizing spell the group has lived under, at which these worn demoralized beings, sending up mute hallelujahs, troop out to a world which has been forced, despite its natural concern, to respect the taboo that has stopped all help at the gate of the mansion's grounds. The conclusion is brilliantly managed as a Mass is offered up by this rich fashionable set in thanks for their deliverance. Then the bigger trap snaps shut and quickly we see machine guns keeping off those who wish to brave the taboo from outside. You're right, gentle reader! The cathedral has become the site of a new self-induced (?) concentration camp. One wonders just what political force has intervened *in behalf of* this new greater taboo . . . But Buñuel's contribution to atomic-age hysteria is unchallengeable. With its cooling nudes, its ambivalently symbolic knives and intrusive cameras, its stark liaisons between Madison Avenue and Greenwich Village, its seeping radioactivity and the optimistic space of astronauts, its fusions of past and future by the grace of drugs, its idiot's laughter in the throats of the elite—this, our stifling paranoid world is caught by Buñuel in the act of . . . ex-

120 panding.

A Modern Fable: Miracle in Milan

The problem of meaning becomes unusually delicate in our time because of complex factors: not only the international situation with its primarily material outlook, but also the situation of man, the decline of whose moral and religious standards have weakened both the reading of motive (good or bad) and the reading of destiny (good or bad). "Is humanity essentially good?" is a question almost as old as the hills. Various religions and philosophies have had various answers; moreover, there is the pristine problem of God, especially what role He plays in the control of human affairs. Then, modern psychology, having immensely widened the field of moral behavior by attaching to it the unconscious realm of motive, has done much to complicate the values of good and bad—notably, of course, with respect to criminals and their motives.

The brief paragraph above might seem to represent all our problems today as a planetary society. The perpetual "what" and the perpetual "how" still remain in vital suspense—I mean for all who care to think seriously about man and his works. Among those film-makers who seem to care, today, is the team of Zavattini and De Sica, which gave us the outstanding film, *Bicycle Thief.* Their film of some years ago, *Miracle in Milan,* was designed apparently to enrich what might be considered a realm of much deficit in modern art: the allegorical tale which simplifies existence to an obvious set of values and furnishes man and his destiny with a single archetype.

Modern poetry, we might note, has felt unable to do exactly this. I think anyone, who claimed that the righteous skepticism and forlorn faith of Eliot's *Waste Land* is still the measure of spiritual reality for our time, would have a highly plausible argument. Consider, too, that the drama wishing to be intellectually serious has tended to show us the dark side of men's moral struggles: to emphasize (as Pirandello did prototypically) the *quandary* of man rather than his *certainty*. Modern novels have followed suit, and, like Céline's, have been grossly cynical, or surrendered to intellectual paradox. The encyclopedic novelist, Romains, at the end of his grand sequence, leaves mankind stranded between two philosophic views, the Apollonian and Promethean, metaphorically locked in struggle like two battling gods. For him, human destiny ends up discernibly nowhere.

On seeing *Miracle in Milan,* then, one might well ask, after the first few moments, why De Sica and Zavattini should have chosen to depict the human scene with such an outdated mythological formula, combining fairy-tale literalness with a very recognizable Redeemer-myth, and attaching it obviously to modern scenes and conditions. But recount a fable, doubtless, is what they systematically have done. A person called "Toto the Good" is its hero. Toto is a familiar clown's name. But this Toto is totally *good* rather than totally *funny.* In fact, his characterization is utter and obvious: he is the symbol of man's natural innocence.

I think the greatest difficulty faced by De Sica and Zavattini in their chosen task was that of making Toto convincing in the one indispensable way he should have been convincing; *i.e.,* his eternal authenticity and primacy *in nature.* In a Christian-Judaic world, he inherits Jesus' prerogatives of wisdom, kindness, and miracles. And yet he is far less authoritative than Jesus, early in life, became. He does not have Jesus' anger, nor is he conscious of his destiny till it is literally bestowed on him by the spirit of his dead foster mother, who comes down from heaven to give him, in a moment of great social peril, the magic Dove. He is quite irresponsible, in any intellectual sense, for the magic deeds he performs by holding out the Dove in his hand. He is, in fact, as dazed as the poverty-ridden community he suddenly benefits, and in the midst of his official miracle-making he forgets everything else to enjoy the blossoming of his love for the little servant girl who adores him. His earthly destiny is to save his community from those who persecute them, specifically now from the rich landowner who wants to push the squatters off his property as soon as oil is discovered there. Toto almost succeeds, but finally the best he can do is to deliver them from the prospect of jail by leading them up to heaven—and if not to heaven, where?—on flying broomsticks.

Toto's personality, as rendered in the movie, should be closely observed, for it holds the key to any inward consistency the film may have. His resemblance, and the resemblance of his deeds, to such comedians as Chaplin, Harry Langdon, Jimmy Savo, and their deeds, are unmistakable; and especially so, of course, to the fable-making of Chaplin in his later art. Most of the inventions in *Miracle in Milan* are stock comic situations which go back to a theater antedating even Chaplin's first movies. But several great differences are notable of Toto in relation to the comedy-film heroes who preceded him. Above all, the very mask of his face: largish, mature, paradoxically aquiline. Absence of grotesque make-up in Toto's mask is one important element. Not merely is his face unchildlike, neither is it reinforced with the artful make-up of the early Charlie or Harry Langdon or Jimmy Savo. I pick these three because it is they who have exploited best on the screen or the stage a childlike innocence; indeed, who are responsible for the archetypal image, in American theater, of the child-man.

a modern fable: miracle in milan

The artifice of Charlie and the others served a special function; it not only characterized them, it *individualized* them. Indeed, it made them alien from almost everything around them, even from their own groups; they made alliances, usually, only with other individuals (as a rule, a woman). Think of Charlie in a flophouse, and you see him isolated amid his own economic class. Certain phases of the allegory are very clear; for example, Toto symbolically takes on the physical flaws and inadequacies of others—a squint, shortness of stature—by naïvely mimicking them. Also, he is a leader and a builder—as much a Moses as a Jesus. The Judaic element of the Redeemer myth should not be overlooked; if Moses is found as an abandoned infant amid bulrushes, Toto is thus found in a cabbage patch. The timeless and placeless Hooverville of the squatters is the wilderness out of which Toto makes a city, with even a statue in its public square.

When Charlie wished to place his traditional tramp in a contemporary and consciously social perspective, he made him an ordinary worker, and his escapes from reality remained chiefly imaginary: wish fulfillment escapes. Charlie never became a savior of society (much less his own savior) and when he did impersonate a savior, he was a fraud: the Hitler parody of the double role in *The Great Dictator*. Charlie's clown remained an individual. And if other fine comedians revealed the same type of lovable simpleton, the universality they all achieved was the universal model of a type-personality. Not so Toto, about whom there is a curious "naturalness" of personality that coincides with the absence on him of clownish make-up or costume properties. At the same time, however, that Toto is a *naturalized clown* he is also an *abstracted personality*, and as such, his "universality" has been dangerously simplified; dangerously so, that is, as tempting our incredulity.

Of what reality in human nature is Toto supposed to convince us? Apparently of its basic goodness, that very thing which appeared in the title of Romains' extensive novel. Toto is among "the men of good will." He is, indeed, good will's rudimentary incarnation. Now the important statement which De Sica and Zavattini seem to have made in regard to the good will of human nature is that it is fairly close to pathological simple-mindedness; it is completely non-intellectual. This seems a pretty big and pretty positive judgment. And here the role of the supernatural in this movie should be defined. Toto is only supernatural by being *supernaturally simple-minded:* a trait to be connected with the personality of his foster mother, who is extraordinarily infantile (at times she "mouths" like a baby) even for an old woman in her "second childhood."

There are symbols in the early part of the movie which, in this regard, seem to me actually metaphoric. Toto, while a foundling and thus unrelated in blood to his foster mother, takes on her infantilism as a permanent trait. Moreover, she is the medium of the magic property, the Dove, about which Toto is careless after using it. He is so much "out of this world" that he is no proper caretaker of magic within this world. The apotheosis of the climax is therefore consistent: as a Redeemer he can only offer his people the redemption

123

of the Afterworld. But still another thing operates as a significant factor. When Toto's foster mother, on her deathbed, makes him recite equations from the multiplication table, the size of the equations steadily diminish till "3×3" is reached. Then, when he has become the guiding spirit of his Hooverville, he changes the conventional street names to multiplication formulas, calling one of them "Via 1×1." It seems very likely that this going backward to the beginning signifies a starting over again for mankind itself, perhaps to the very beginning of time; not merely to "Anno Domini," the year of the Redeemer's birth, but to the origin of the human progenitors, Adam and Eve ("1×1"), to whom, in terms of time, grandmother and grandchild alike would be as children.

A turn of the plot, reminiscent of this type of comic stories comes when Toto's servant-girl sweetheart pursues the patrol wagons full of squatters in order to return the lost Dove to Toto, so that he can liberate himself and his people. A second time in the film, then, a female character is the vehicle, if not the wielder, of the magic. Especially in the light of De Sica's and Zavattini's previous film, this should be read, I feel, as a matriarchal prejudice on their part. We saw, in *Bicycle Thief*, how church, police, and trade union—all patriarchally dominated—failed to assist the worker looking for his stolen bicycle, sometimes even provided obstacles. This gives a certain point to the fact that in *Miracle in Milan*, it is God's angels who steal the Dove from Toto; thus, the "jealous" patriarchal supervision from heaven *limits* Toto's earthly effectiveness.

Curiously suggestive about the plot of *Bicycle Thief* was the machinery by which the worker catches the bicycle thief and is then effectually tempted to steal a bicycle himself, thus automatically taking on all thieves' guilt and purging himself of his moral anxiety. It is the impulse to consult the female fortune-teller that puts him in real proximity with the thief, for immediately after leaving her with her cryptic reply hanging in his mind, he sees the thief on the street outside, chases him, and traps him in the whorehouse where he has sought refuge. The realm of women rather than the realm of men yields him the object he seeks, which is really the thief rather than the bicycle, for only by becoming a thief himself, and being forgiven as the bicycle's owner forgives him, can he learn the lesson of human frailty and charity which it is his destiny to learn.

I infinitely prefer De Sica's worker who is *naturally simple* to De Sica's simpleton who is *supernaturally simple*. This may be a personal prejudice. But I also think that *Bicycle Thief* is a much more eloquent, much truer, work of art. Its sympathy with common humanity seems much less pretentious than does that of *Miracle in Milan*, if only because *Miracle in Milan*, as I have said, makes (or seems to make) a final moral judgment of the best in mankind. The *envoi*, rendered verbally at the movie's final shot, when we see all Hooverville flying into the clouds on broomsticks, looks forward to "a world in which 'Good morning' really means 'Good morning.' " Therefore the moral intention of the film cannot be missed. The most important thing in life is man's good

124

will toward man, even if, to support this judgment, the downtrodden and deprived must be consoled by such fantastic myths as that embodied in this movie.

Finally, *Miracle in Milan* is only a portrait of the myth-making faculty itself. Toto is but the incarnation of the good-boy-in-the-fairy-tale translated to something close to the conditions governing all those rendered helpless by their innocence of evil. Thus, it is by a negative route that Toto becomes merely human as well as merely good. His humanity exists through a defect: *he does not hate*. His instinct is for cooperation on an absolute plane. When he is enough of an individual to forget his mission, as during the courtship sequence, it is his sweetheart who reminds him of it and returns his gift to him.

Does this mean that man is to look to a mother-goddess of the future rather than to the father-god of the past? One might reason so. Indeed, this seems the true ideology of the film: the evil of the world is the aggressiveness concentrated in the masculine personality; to be good, the male must sacrifice his so-called political wisdom with its ambiguous good-evil nature and be purified by the spirit of the female, which is maternal goodness unqualified. This should be his true "politics," no matter how many times it fails, for only by persisting in his instinctive goodness can man ever create a truly good society. The known ideology closest to the implied philosophy of De Sica's and Zavattini's allegory is, I imagine, Gandhi's. It is the political weapon of passive resistance: the magic of an incarnation of the spirit uncompromisingly dedicated to peace.

We see, in *Miracle in Milan*, that the Dove is instrumental only in a *defensive*, and what amounts to a *sham*, war, and that it is ultimately effectual only in delivering humanity to its sublimal, not its mundane, destiny. The film's *envoi* might imply only a token hopefulness; again, it might imply that earthly progress is achieved in the recurrences of the heavenly Redeemer. *Miracle in Milan* is not sure enough as a work of art to make clear its final message. As to its sexual implications in the personality of the "Redeemer," I think the film bears all the marks of an emasculated mental and moral operation. It quite lacks the positive character of a moral allegory such as *Gulliver's Travels*. Too many ambiguous social tags are involved; for instance, the resemblance between Toto and Mussolini in physical terms is too obvious to be overlooked. Thus the personality of the Redeemer is shown as compromised, vulnerable—as, indeed, an historic question mark.

On the Cult of Displaced Laughter

It has been more than half a century since the medium of moving photography was able to furnish one of its first thrills of eroticism, *The Kiss* (which lasted a minute), and one of its first thrills of fantasy, *A Trip to the Moon*. Eroticism and Fantasy are the twinlike realms of filmic eloquence chosen respectively by the editors of two recently published, historically impressive books of "stills."[1] These volumes are notable for both exhaustive research among the films of the world and the air given the movies of being something that shifts easily and amusingly back and forth from horror to lust, fantasy to fun, and science to sex. Of course, observers of society on one side and cinéastes from the other, with plain movie fans between, have long been familiar with the phenomena rather elegantly exploited by the two albums, which originate in France and whose captions are French. One finds that a little French, even of the college-learned kind, goes a long way through these pictorial labyrinths, even a bit farther than necessary to grasp the "hidden message" of a displaced laughter.

Perhaps the unique, the precious, thing about all laughter is that it provides in any age the perfect key to society's various cults, whether as open and simple as those of Marilyn Monroe and Mae West, Garbo and Dietrich, or as closed and complex as those signalized by the Robot-Queen of the old German film, *Metropolis*, who is readily identifiable in these Gravesian days as the White Goddess in her "terrible aspect." Encyclopedic example: the "still" showing Mr. Hyde—of Dr. Jekyll fame—assaulting a prostitute: the players are Fredric March and Miriam Hopkins. They wear—one supposes involuntarily, which makes it all the funnier—identical expressions in which "lust" meets and marries indistinguishably with "horror." Incidentally, one also detects the bad Roman imitations of the Greek tragic and comic masks. The movies, whatever their passing virtues and faults, may be depended upon to remind us of certain popular fantasies, certain vestigial myths, which find it as

[1] *L'Erotisme au Cinéma*. Par Lo Duca. Jean-Jacques Pauvert, Editeur. Pauvert. Paris. *Le Fantastique au Cinéma*. Par Michel Laclos. Jean-Jacques Pauvert, Editeur. Pauvert, Paris.

hard to die as Frankenstein himself. Haunted, hard-working Hollywood lately came up with a "teen-age Frankenstein." Though not so distinguished as his cultural daddy, he at least proved the survival of his line. At the moment I write, still another cult-pregnant Frankenstein item is going the rounds of the New York film houses.

If culture, in its vast way, is timeless and all too fluid, cults in their triviality tend to be neat, timely and assessable. Yet they have a reflexive way of coming back from the grave. After Frankenstein's monster first established himself on the world screen as the more or less biological bastard of science and sexiness, it was decided (shades of the caged ape!) that he needed a mate; hence: *Bride of Frankenstein.* There is a very funny "still" in the fantasy album showing Boris Karloff as the monster and Elsa Lanchester—of all people!—as his bride. Scars of surgical zeal near their necks plainly reveal the hideous truth: both are resurrected from the morgue or a similar repository. Their expressions show more astonishment than erotic susceptibility: a bias which might reasonably be inferred from their late ordeals; neither expected to be given another chance at "love" after their exits from this Vale of Tears. Part of our laughter, even part of our chill (automatic in all perishable flesh) is certainly owed to the fact that men and women, in and out of the acting profession, get their faces lifted and their features changed; that is, submit to anesthesia while operated on for the purpose of restoring or acquiring charm, beauty, and/or youth.

The impact of tragedy is relatively timeless—as the revival of Greek classic drama in our era demonstrates—yet the impact of comedy, much more qualified by passing social humors, varies widely throughout the history of the arts. The question might well be proposed, considering how moody society has been since the start of the century, whether the movies may not have bound up their own nature with the audience's nature, and in Pirandellian key shuttled reality with fantasy as glibly as comedy with tragedy. The appearance of the French picture books, obviously signifying a polite pornography of the cultivated, may indicate merely the responsiveness of a single sophisticated cult, one of all too subtly displaced laughter. According to the key response of this audience (go to the nearest art-film house to hear it), love and the imagination, at the shortest possible notice, are subject to being swept into the realm of science fantasy and burlesque sex by one ill-timed guffaw. Now is this cult audience simply effete, morally exhausted? Is it, by and large, paranoid? Or is it, perhaps, becoming part of the Existentialist milieu of "strangers" to existence—and thus strangers to aesthetic as well as to moral values?

The canned economy involved with a notably canned product may reveal something very important about it. The movie convention known as the "trailer" seeks to condense into a few minutes of intense animation the most "salable" elements of the coming program and so produces shameless vulgarization in an object of already compromised dignity. The trailer is in atrocious taste. But grim, silent revulsion is not necessarily the mood in which it is received. I have even heard connoisseurs declare that seeing the trailer makes **127** it unnecessary to see the film. However true this may be, art-film houses are by no means averse to letting their choicest exhibits be seen in the trailer's inflammatory spotlight. The other evening, I sat in a theater where the trailer for a frankly sensational, though presumably serious, sex romance was disclosed in briefs, as usual, as soon as the feature had flickered off. Its corny commentary, together with the obliquely suggestive sequence of shots, held the audience in perpetual uproar for its duration. One could assume that this was a cult phenomenon consciously sparked by a few ultra-aesthetes in the audience, but suppose, assuming quite another perspective, one could take it as a sound judgment by society's deep good sense? These days the movies, even a large proportion of the foreign ones, begin by wanting sex to look both sexy and amusing, and through systematic vulgarity end by making it look even funnier than intended. Possibly an inexorably moral logic, of which these two picture books are simply a veracious symptom, has been long at work; the Cult of Displaced Laughter is based on certain stark truths of modern society: chief among them is the great disillusionment with institutions—with comedy and tragedy as with democracy and dictatorship.

In such a despair of the cultural economy, what is universally recognized as commercial vulgarity is to be as heartily enjoyed—according to rules of the Cult of Displaced Laughter—as high tragedy or high comedy, and the cultist tends not to care which grand aesthetic principle, precisely, is being vitiated. Perhaps the Tired Aesthete has replaced the Tired Business Man more profoundly, and for more decades, than has come to particular notice. At least, stoic submission to vulgarity would seem the aesthete's only alternative to excessively sophisticated howling at it. On the current off-Broadway stage, the rising star of Existentialist comedy has almost risen to middle-brow popularity; so nearly so, that those who cherish the true aesthetic reaction are heard to complain, between acts of a Beckett or Ionesco comedy, that the audience is laughing "at the wrong places."

Are these delicate handlers of aesthetic conscience not being reactionary? Theater comedy may have come to the point where the audience—regardless of the creator's intention—is always right. An anecdote will serve to illustrate the trend I mean. Tennessee Williams is a notable American playwright who cannot have failed to be as sensitive to transoceanic influences as foreign audiences have been to certain of his plays. An old tale is told of the Chicago première of *The Rose Tattoo* (later a screen vehicle for Anna Magnani, for whom it was written): the lead actress lamented backstage, during the performance, that the audience was laughing at her serious lines. "If they laugh," the playwright is reported soberly to have reassured her, "it's a comedy." Now there are, of course, the hybrid theatrical genres that perhaps Euripides himself (with such works as *Alcestis* and *Helen*) may be the first to have invented as primordial parent of the Cult of Displaced Laughter. But the ready chameleonism of Mr. Williams' reply to his lead seems compelling: no aesthetic logic-

128

chopping when it comes to audience response! *The Rose Tattoo*, despite its moments both sordid and romantic, was thereafter to be a comedy.

Could there be something global about the contemporary emulsion of the art genres? Subtlety all to one side as a sophisticates' squabble, the death of old-fashioned slapstick in the movies was the end of a broad genre far more elementary than "Aristophanic" laughter; its requiem has already been sung in a historic visual anthology called *The Golden Age of Comedy*. Even the fey ingenuity of the Marx brothers, whose relation to Surrealism was always plain, finally yielded to time. Today the inherently verbal character of radio as transmitted to television has promoted the non-visual elements of this newest of folk media, so that "sight gags" by no means now reign in TV studios. As for slapstick movement, as glorified by the vanished silent-screen comedians, it is a museum curio, significantly relished only by cinéastes and nostalgists.

On the radio, comedy became soap opera; now on television, gags mixed with personalities have finally almost pushed the comedy of movement and the clown's deformity off the scene of the popular arts. It is time for every celebrity to seem as ridiculous as Garbo in the very last film she made, *Two-Faced Woman*, little more than a charade of the two personalities which box-office sentiment had compelled her to develop. If Dietrich, fresh from resurrective techniques, is still "delicious," she is deliciously funny rather than deliciously glamorous: a sort of "retouched" photograph of Mae West. Glamor, to be sure, is still pay-dirt—yet now it is best that it be pay-dirt with cannonading of the vocal cords. Tallulah Bankhead apparently was judged neither fantastic nor erotic enough for inclusion in our two picture books but she is a classic case in point. She was a star who vulgarized herself with an honest good-will, and for years—after failure in Hollywood and on Broadway—was a radio "comic" glorying in her sarcastic fate.

Kidding itself has always been the privilege of the upper classes, professional and social. Has it at last become their necessity—and is the truly cultivated class among those for whom the classic privilege has become a "necessary" luxury? Top-level sophisticates can moon over the aesthetic grandeurs of silent movies and bygone glamor boys and girls as much as do cinéastes, for whom the cult-reaction is more naturally poker-faced. Garbo in *Camille*, John Barrymore in *Beau Brummel* or *Moby Dick*, the "great" slapstick artists of the screen, have disappeared only to become classics of the heart as of the museum. Speaking *nostalgically*, it is our grandfathers and grandmothers in general that we regret; not just their aesthetic responses and opportunities to enjoy a perished art of the theater, but also their clothes, their relative moral simplicity, and above all the dignity, along with charming quaintness, which their traditional images can inspire in our feelings. The French albums of eroticism and fantasy roll up nostalgia and the latest in science fiction into, so to speak, one endless film-strip so that we get the impression of a newsreel documenting What Fun—from Cocteau to Comedy regardless of date-of-issue—the Movies Can Be. However, after the first few chortles and giggles, one grows a little grim, even

129

stoic. Exposed on the title page of the erotic album is something which unites Alcibiades at his blasphemous tricks with Daumier at his: a puritanical gentle-man in the garb of an undertaker reaches up to affix a fig leaf to an antique statue.

This naïf-sophisticated image is taken from an equally naïf-sophisticated Experimental film by a middle-aged member of the avant-garde school. It was placed thus strategically in the album partly because of its cutely insinuating view, which is angled from the ground. "Worm's-eye view" is closely related to "Earth Mother's view." Maybe it is chthonic laughter to which the cult leaders and art albums of the film world invite us: that chthonic laughter that belongs to Hades and the grave as well as to the womb-from-which-all-things-come. This would explain why the French albums seem so successfully designed to companion each other. Yet an aura of impurity hangs about this Madame Tussaud's of the movie cliques. One finds oneself supersatiated after hardly more than tasting the fun. The comedy rigidifies into the poker-faced aspect of Samuel Beckett's stage, where it is not that the pathos is too much for laughter—if only because the audience laughs "at the wrong places"—but that the comedy as such is in bad taste. It is the ironic gusto of bad taste that feeds the Cult of Displaced Laughter.

The Atomophobe: A New Culture Hero

A man wakes up one morning to find himself an obnoxious insect, one frequenting domestic interiors; he cannot go to work, he becomes a tragic plague to his family, and he realizes an external, irremediable form has been given his underground shrinking from his common daily life. His is a human doom for which as yet no super-insecticide has been invented. The story, of course, is Kafka's *Metamorphosis*, its protagonist the author's legendary hero of Alienation. Or, a man finds himself arrested for a crime whose nature continues to be concealed from him after his apprehension while his trial for it seems indefinitely postponed; mechanically, he goes about seeking to "arrange" his exoneration along sub-rosa official paths: another hero of Kafka's, this one as inextricably trapped as the insect hero. His name in the novels, *The Castle* and *The Trial,* is K.; throughout *The Castle,* he tries to obtain that from which he is suddenly detached in *The Trial:* a job. Thus what is called "alienation" might be termed in general a Totality Atmosphere connoting a radically *negative* phase of ordinary human existence. K. is never *in* a job; though technically he may once have occupied it, it has no true existence, in the sense of possession or duration. To all visible intents and purposes in Kafka's fiction, K. *never* occupies a job—the nearest he comes to doing so is as Karl, the immigrant who becomes an itinerant worker in the earliest novel, *Amerika.* Essentially, Karl belongs to the "eternally unemployed," being symbolic of the permanent statistical margin of the actually unemployed.

Another Totality Atmosphere in modern fiction is Proust's. Perhaps a third is to be detected in Camus' *The Stranger,* where a spontaneous homicide is portrayed as quite without conscious or particular motive. What can be generally said of such "atmospheres"? They are, to be sure, *subjective fictions* only because so exclusively subjective and extreme in feeling, for they relate to very recognizable experiences in human society. And yet, as planetary life proceeds from day to day, paced by conventional ambitions and preoccupations, such moral reflexes as are found dominating the lives of Kafka's K. and Proust's Marcel—whose Total Recall ritualizes the past as an imaginative absolute—

are completely absorbed into society's vast normal rhythm. All the heroes I have mentioned are symbolic extremes of human behavior and human motives —in fine, of human consciousness. They are curiously brought into line with a new type of conscious extreme that *indicates* a new Totality Atmosphere without actually projecting it. This has occurred in a new Japanese movie, *I Live in Fear*, whose hero sustains a state of mind which, grasped as it is here in relation to the real world, makes him appear in much the same light as Kafka's insect hero: he is a plague and a freak whose relation to suppressed or unconscious factors of ordinary psychic life is all too close and pointed.

The theme of the movie, as it were, creeps up on one. Unfortunately, American audiences may never see it since distributors, for obvious reasons, have declined to touch it even though virtually all the rest of the "civilized world" has seen it. The filmic scene against which the movie's credits are projected is a mural of ordinary people, probably office workers, going to and fro at a big city cross-roads; though the locale is Tokyo, or some other Japanese metropolis, the scene might be Times Square for all that faces or clothes, at the given distance, tell us. Japanese physiognomy, indeed, is so widely ranged among old and young that, even as we get into the film, a curious "internationalism" stamps its look. The dramatic situation to which we are introduced is also notably universal in type: a corridor in a family court where the litigants in a dispute are caught in the midst of their humiliating dilemma. A modern patriarch—his fan the only positive "Japanese" thing about him—is being accused of "quasi-incompetency" by his wife and grown son and daughter. His alleged incompetency, we soon learn, consists of only one thing, but it is as effectual as the physical transformation of Kafka's hero, Gregor, into an insect pest: he is an Atomophobe.

Dreading the next war as a universal destruction by radioactivity, the patriarch, a well-to-do factory owner, has recently designed his life as a field of preventive operations to guarantee himself and his family against what he presumes as the coming general annihilation. His first idea has been an underground house, and as the movie opens, he has already executed and abandoned this plan because tests have shown the structure would be vulnerable to radioactivity. The expense has been enormous, and the plan especially objectionable to his wife and son since the underground colony would include not merely his legitimate family but also two mistresses and his illegitimate offspring. Obviously, from one angle, the situation involves that human "remnant" which has been the focus of imaginary tales of earthly destruction ushering in an ideal, or utopian, society. However, this movie never projects its Totality Atmosphere in such ways but is confined to insinuating it through the isolated case of this headstrong Atomophobe. He is a Camuseque "stranger," dedicated to committing a potential, though undeliberate, crime. In substance, this "crime" is reluctantly recognized by the presiding judges and his advisers (a lawyer and a dentist) as disruption of the existent and desirable psychic order of society in the present world situation; this is a basic order to be called, perhaps, a pseudo-peace since the international "peace," beyond question, is an ever-threatened, if temporarily working, status quo. If this status quo were not preserved in the "total" sense, social panic would automatically result.

What has actually happened to the private and individual psychic order of this Japanese hero, so decisively alienated from the pseudo-peace of the planet? An insanity test is not even required in his case: he would be sure to emerge from it with flying colors. In fact, his poise and reasonableness, in his critical and humiliating situation, much impress the three arbiters who listen to his defense *in camera*. They are shaken when he tells them it is *they*, not himself, who are "cowards" because they sit calmly, passively, awaiting the doom which *he* visualizes so clearly. It cannot help occurring to these astute and equable gentlemen that, once granted the acute anticipatory vision of the defendant, it would be merely "logical" to behave just as he is doing; what accounts for his "vision," of course, is neither logic nor reason, but emotion and imagination: the "accident" of his private temperament. The legal panel is given further pause by the fact that, at this point, the alleged semilunatic does not plan to build a space ship and escape to the moon or anything of that audacious variety. All he desires his family to do is to emigrate with him to South America, which he has decided is the only continent having a plausible chance to escape the fatal consequences of an atomic war. Having already set in motion a deal to exchange his factory for a farm in Brazil, he has forced his rebellious family's hand; hence, their lawsuit is a truly desperate measure.

From the average psychological viewpoint, the old man is a supercrank whose obsession tends to overthrow his family's whole order and happiness. Finally, the case is decided against him, and he is prohibited from using his money to forward the emigration scheme. Now he is a moral leper as palpably as the verminized hero of *Metamorphosis* and he becomes a dreaded stranger in his own house. If Gregor Samsa *felt* like vermin, and for this reason alone, apparently, wakes up one morning to find himself one, this Japanese wakes up one morning to find himself an "incompetent" because of a parallel imaginative obsession; though not incarcerated as mentally ill, he is a hopelessly stigmatized individual. The hydrogen bomb which remains a present fact to him is, by token of the legal verdict, a lunatic's myth to which he evidently clings and which forms, in his presence, a Totality Atmosphere. . . . What distinguishes this psychic atmosphere is its time-relation. While Marcel's is oriented to the *past* and K.'s to the *present*, the factory owner's is oriented to the *future*. His is the Totality Atmosphere of *Anticipation*. Being, however, a future possibility rather than a present fact, "Anticipation" does not become a *total* subjective atmosphere—such as the corresponding states in Proust and Kafka —till the court's decision is delivered against the patriarch; then, what was reasonable precaution against the evidence of the imagination becomes, naked and absolute, the evidence of the imagination itself. . . .

The poor man goes around all too consciously wrapped in his disgraced aura of "mad" eccentricity. His condition is climaxed in a last hysterical plea to his **133** assembled relatives—no longer dependents but their own masters—to obey his will and buy the Brazilian farm. His pathetic abjection, significantly, touches none of them but his helpless teen-age daughter; after collapsing, he creeps onto his couch, that night, a tragically numb and defeated man. But he lies awake eavesdropping on the family's plans and gets a fugitive inspiration. When all are asleep, he manages to set fire to the factory, hoping by this "strategy" to compel them to fall in with his design.

Inevitably, the only result is a taste of the final calamity which he wishes to spare himself and his family, and just as inevitably he exhibits acute signs of mental breakdown as the logical outcome of his cumulative hysteria. His workers, beside the ruined factory, demand of him to say what will become of *them*. His paranoid reasoning does not fail him: "Come with us to Brazil!" he cries out. Now, of course, his destination is not Brazil but the insane asylum, where we next see him being visited by the dentist who sat on the panel that condemned him. This man has been the one most doubtful of the verdict rendered by the panel but has bowed to the arguments of his colleagues. The patriarch, reading cross-legged on his bed in his private cell, at first takes no notice of his visitor; then he turns casually from his book and asks him: "By the way, what happened to the earth?"

The poetic effect is a little breathtaking and makes one regret that the movie itself, though well done in many ways, is not closer to being an artistic masterpiece. After all, as I said, it connotes, rather than projects, a Totality Atmosphere. Still, as the confirmed paranoiac walks to his window, he catches sight of the sun shining at him through the frosted glass and, exclaiming, identifies it as the earth aflame in its death throes. This is at least a glimpse of Total Anticipation: that mirage of terror which is patted to sleep, night after night, under more than one comfortable pillow. Here is the kind of hero whose authenticity cannot be doubted and yet whose phenomenon is a surprise—almost (this explains the reluctance of the film distributors) an unpardonable "indiscretion."

It is just as easy to imagine in passing the Atomophobe hero as it is hard to consider him an "Existential" fact such as Kafka's insect hero. This is the difficulty experienced by the patriarch's judges: he seems to belong in the world of fiction rather than in that of fact, for in the latter he ultimately must be classified as "incompetent"; that is, as *totally* alienated. Taking the objective stance toward potential psychopathology, the movie concentrates on the realistic "other side" of science fiction's utopian outlook on scientific progress. The man-made satellites that have circled our globe possess, everyone knows, sinister as well as benign connotations for futurity. In focusing a hero's consciousness on the sinister outlook—in presenting the hydrogen bomb as an overwhelming psychic fact to a single private individual—this Japanese film adds a provoking cultural statistic to those implicit in the fictive atmospheres of Proust and Kafka. It is precisely *lack of confidence in the future* that renders the Totality Atmospheres of the Recall and the Alienation heroes what they are and so it renders that of this Anticipation hero. Beneath the surface of the Japanese court's logic is the radical psychic principle of global moral necessity: a wholly tacit confidence in the future must exist to keep the world running whether or not the future does hold an all-out atomic war. This confidence would never be put in question except by one of nature's well-known, if inexplicable, aberrations such as the Atomophobe, which perhaps is too portentous, too pathological, a term for this hero. Maybe he should be considered our century's first *truly serious* worrier. In any case, his motif of Total Anticipation makes him a new culture hero, one that should not be dismissed as merely "morbid."

Movies and the Human Image

One wonders if photography competes with art in the way that—as E. E. Cummings once poignantly noted—poetry competes with elephants and El Greco. The consciousness of such a hypothesis may depend on the development of one's competitive sense. Intellectually, our more or less remote ancestors had to deal, when deciding any great moral issue (including the aesthetic), with fewer factors than we. A "global" community of nations has meant, whatever the specific problem, that more factors must be considered, all at once, on parallel levels. So asking the question "Have the movies prolonged the life of the classic human image?" I am aware that one might attack the problem by many routes, some deceptively simple and yet all really devious. One presumes that the issue is vital, if not to the movies, at least to art. Perhaps the movies—aside from the avant-garde ranks, which are very, very small—don't care whether their imagery has an aesthetic status, so-called, and perhaps abstract artists, for their part, are by now so convinced of their canon's public and financial triumph that the notion of the movies' doing anything in our time to revive the prestige of the classic human image seems frivolous—if not downright irrelevant.

Merely to equate the terms in my formulation brings up startling contradictions within the formulation. First of all: Is an equivalence between photography and classical art not far more "statistical" and "documentary" than aesthetic? For instance, what vital, artistically critical relation has the conventional image of the movies to an antique sculptural frieze or to Poussin's version of such a frieze? This objecting query might emanate from the admirers of Poussin as well as from true film devotées, who would urge that the photographic image per se is what holds the movies back. Indeed, to consider the atmospheric effects possible to modern photography, as well as the distortion possible through objective and laboratory means, is to conclude that an equation of photography with "classic" form represents an old-fashioned prejudice for which commercial filmdom alone is to blame. Through sheer movement—with its attendant blur of instantaneous imagery and the rapidity producing a purely psychic "blur"—highly expressionistic, no less than surrealistic, effects have been, and are, obtained by imaginative movie-makers.

Where does this reflection leave the present equation between photography and classic art? Just about no place inevitable. Granting that, with imaginative photography and its increasing technical resources, a highly realistic, stylized imagery is obtainable for the film screen, a stubborn element persists in the aesthetic equation I have proposed: an element against the grain. Abstract painting of the non-objective kind seriously differs from all filmic imagery except that which (sometimes without photography) exactly and exclusively imitates such painting; that is, non-objective painting disposes of literal and unmistakable referents to human experience. A seeming paradox naturally follows: howsoever, this is not to say that non-objective abstractionism is an art wholly *outside* human experience. An important point is to be observed of extreme abstract painting from Mondrian to Rothko, Reinhardt and company: it tends to offer viewers not, precisely speaking, a *picture*, but rather a *creative décor* of the mural type.

A Mondrian or a late Rothko, purified of figure and primarily "inactive," remains pure design—though design-atmosphere would be a better term— because late Rothkos look like tranquilly pulsing atmospheres of color. This pure design is intended as the modulation of a wall, whether private or museum wall, and is the *dernier cri* of interior design. Its pretension to being art, rather than mere decoration, is based on a quite simple idea: an aesthetic image need not be a statement concerning something external to itself; it may "state" itself as any other object does. This theoretical position has animated the practice of pure-abstract art from the beginning, when Kandinsky, Mondrian, Pevsner, Gabo, Malevich and Delaunay talked like philosophers and advocated, in one respect or another, a new "realism." Non-objective art ("extreme" or "pure" abstraction) is a statement *period* (.) Supposedly, it evokes a "mood," a psychic vibration of some kind. But, thus, it enters life like any other motivation, cause or visual happening—as would a meteor from outer space or a perfect stranger on the doorstep. The said meteor and the said stranger may affect one's life or not affect it at all. Like Kilroy, it "was here," and sometimes one remembers it, encounters its mark, or prefers to keep it, even falling in love with it. . . .

Now the only sensible, irreducible and unavoidable thing to say about this conception of the work of art as a "non-objective" phenomenon, which is really objective after all, is that it produces a gaping hole in the tradition of human culture—which it tries to fill up exactly as though it had made an actual hole in a wall. In my aforesaid proposition, therefore, the issue concerning the photographic in relation to the classic human image devolves not upon the question of style, or so-called distortion in art, but upon the question of humanity's ability to produce and assess works of art through conscious means having nothing to do with the necessary dependence of form upon content; nothing to do with the classic aesthetic dualism of form united with its content. By its nature, photography possesses a highly prejudiced standpoint on this issue. **137**

As many have already observed, the aesthetic character of the movies *begins* by being so naturalistic, so "documentary," as a notation of life that, among all the arts, the movies evoke the most urgent sense of comparison and contrast with life itself. Film is the art—and this is a pivotal definition—where the finished "form" is the most easily soluble into raw "content" or ingredients of meaning. Both psychologically and technically, the photographic lens is a mirror, even if a sometimes flattering one. For this reason, the relation of photography to the classic human image is simple and direct. Classic Western art evolved through the aesthetic desire to come as close to nature (or "content") as possible while in the same act "idealizing" it: giving it a flattering look (or "form").

Now, if, in time, the idealism of the ancient Greeks produced the aesthetic coldness of Neo-Classicism and its remoteness from common experience—something that was radically challenged by nineteenth-century artists—this became true not because Poussin and David failed to be great painters, but because what they painted, and to some extent how they painted it, became irrelevant and objectionable to a vital social experience composed of various new moral factors: the congruent rise of individualism and the bourgeoisie, the French Revolution, and so on. Yet soon a reaction set in against the nineteenth-century "revolution" in painting. When the Impressionists came along, they seemed quite as disinterested in violent feelings as they were in violent actions. And if the Post-Impressionists, carrying forward Van Gogh's violence through the Fauves, returned to activized brushes and activized feelings, theirs was simply a reaction to a reaction. In fact, when the twentieth-century began, painting was a more or less restless heap of "school" reactions, a heap both topped and toppled, temporally speaking, by the chaotic nihilism of the Dadaists and Surrealists.

All the same, in artists such as Giorgio de Chirico, Jacques Lipchitz and Marcel Duchamp, this century has produced heroic figures who have used art—however debonairly as in the case of the Dada-nurtured Duchamp—as a highly organized aesthetic instrument both creating and criticizing human values. André Breton, the best-known theorist of Surrealism, is notable for his classical poise and his equally classical literary style. After all, nothing in the tradition of classical humanism interdicts violent or positive feelings; all artistic discipline, indeed, requires initiative and decisiveness, which cannot exist without their own driving power. Chirico's art is proof-simple that the style-atmosphere of Greek classicism, the mainstay of the humanist tradition, had a twentieth-century application: was convertible into a new art idiom; his art displays the most serious use of the Surrealist postulate of synthetic vision: the "psychological" as opposed to the "natural" landscape. But when has the painted landscape ever been quite "natural"? Romanticism once had its psychological landscape, and as for the Baroque before that, its landscapes were nothing if not "theatrical."

It may be time to insert the question of why we tend to equate our cultural history with man as specifically the "classic human image." The essence of

138

Christian-pagan idealism is necessarily philosophic and therefore "humanist" in the widest possible as well as the narrowest sense. In this specifically humanist role of classicism, the aesthetic tradition has actually subsumed all "revolutions" and "reactions," Neo-Classicism, Romanticism and Cubism alike. Historically, classicism is nothing but the moral preëminence of Man—man as a theoretically, or "rationally," perfectible if not perfect being. Preferably and conventionally, man is inspired by God, but at least he is given his basic meaning by the ability to reason, to relate himself to gods, other men, and nature as well as to art. All the aesthetic revolutions of "schools," even some in the twentieth-century, have tacitly assumed this "classic" tenet of art.

The Dada-Surrealists, in their animosity against the "conventional" image of man and his world—what roughly may be called the *photographic* image— were attacking not the means of art, but its end; not the image of man and nature in all its variety and possibility, but the lack of imaginative energy with which the classical-humanist tradition was being preserved by the pictorial and literary arts. Even Futurism's violent conversion of the Cubist schema to machine imagery did not suit the Dadaists' revolt; this was because they could sense the academic future of so systematic a formal procedure as Cubism proposed; surely enough, today abstract art has arrived at its own rigid, sterile academism.

It was, then, in behalf of the inherent vitality of classical-humanism that the Dada-Surrealist spirit proceeded with its kudos, its tricks, its shocks and its chef-d'oeuvres—of which certainly Duchamp's great glass, *The Bride Denuded* (*etc.*), owned by the Philadelphia Museum since it acquired the Arensburg Collection, is one of the most important: a combined trick, shock, kudo and chef-d'oeuvre. Here man is insect, mannikin, hieroglyph, and even "thing." What, exactly, does *The Bride* "say"? It says that man exists by showing how very *specially* he *can* exist . . . On the other hand, non-objective art is actually pre-human if post-humanist: the world-without-man—the world that, like original nature, could exist, and did exist, before man; it is a world, moreover, not necessarily implying that crucial evolutionary movement of nature that brought man into being—man, one should add, with all his astonishing ability to transform and "distort" himself and the world around him. . . .

Accordingly, something most significant lies in the fact that, at the same moment that twentieth-century painting was girding itself to make a complete break with representationalism, the "representational" movies came into being and cast their universal public spell. If Surrealist painting and collage, with its supreme dislocation, its fragmented and as it were "paraplegic" world of the senses, was to attack classical humanism, it was to attack its complacency, not its historical roots in man. On the contrary, in embracing the non-representational world, abstract art ultimately took the most radical step possible against human and social consciousness as the cradle, critic and creator of aesthetic values. Hence, automatically, while in a prejudiced and deceptive way, the movies adopted a hostile position toward abstract art, though on a moral rather than an artistic basis; in this distinction within the character of the movies' opposition to abstract art lies the "rub" of complexity and vagueness about the issue I have proposed: whether *as an art* they have prolonged the life of the classical human image. For, as I have said, they can be, and have been, as expressionistic, as highly "formal," even as abstract as they please; the obstacle in the way of their being as much so as they please is not technical limitation, but simply the arbitrary premises of filmdom's highly organized—if now wobbly —commercial art.

One need not stress why these premises are so "arbitrary." The point at issue is why, commercially or not, the movies may be said to take the *aesthetic* side of the classic human image. Let me point out the naïve "magic of effect" that clings to the junkiest movie. The movies' hallucination of reality is a theme to which I have devoted many thousands of words, and always with the assumption that the terms of the formulation, "reality" and "hallucination," have an equal and reflexive weight. *Reality* in the movies reasserts "content" in the classic aesthetic dualism, *hallucination* reasserts "form." What made the timing of the movies' advent so significant was exactly that the whole tradition which a painter such as Ingres had inherited from the Renaissance, and the super-photographic perfection he gave that tradition, was swiftly turning into dull academism, which seemed to the Romantics, and finally the Expressionists and the Cubists, to have a static, unbearably complacent look.

Just at this moment of greatest peril for the classic human image, the mechanism of photography intervened to mock the accumulated craft of the hand and the pencil, the hand and the brush. One might argue that photography—despite its early motives both "aesthetic" and "romantic"—killed academic art; well and good, but suppose it also killed the classic human image? If I think that photography did not do this, but the opposite, *revived* the classic human image, it is only because photography began to move: became the *movies*. Suddenly man's representational image was galvanized, and in this sense human identity in art was given a new meaning through its additional element: *kinesis*. Painting and sculpture "move" in a quite different sense from the cinema. It is instructive that not until after the movies were invented, and had progressed in technique, did the artist's eye, through Futurism, dedicate itself to an isolated "aesthetic" of movement; to a plastic which, in substance, was merely the analysis of optical mechanism made possible by the camera.

Of course, movement in the movies is already—largely owing to the requirements of the commercial product—a monotonous, by no means sufficiently aesthetic, cult. Yet one finds serious theorists of the film almost automatically insisting on the value of movement as such: on broad panoramas and swift changes of the centers of action. To be sure, this is only one of the aesthetic conditioned reflexes of a still young art, an art still naïvely inflamed by the extent to which it surpasses stage action in narrative scope and significance. On one side, the movies challenge the novel in this scope and significance, while on the other they have the literal vision of the stage (and of painting) and at last have assimilated the stage's oral dialogue. But it is fatal to dwell on the achieve-

140

ments of the movies as a "great" synthetic art. Among the manifold attempts to reproduce famous novels and "expand" famous plays on the screen, merely a handful have lacked the most disastrous flaws, and even with these, it would be dangerous to try to prove they deserve to be compared with the originals.

My object here is not to exalt specimens of the film but to hail the movies as the probable savior of the classic human image in our age—certainly, as an aesthetic force which has specifically "prolonged" the life of that image. What academic painting had shown as overrefined and static, the movies began to present as crude if refinable nature and as notably fluid. No art medium can convey so immediate a *sensation* of time in its changes, its whims and provocative shifts, as the movies. And yet, because basically photography remains a mirror (something it is very hard for it not to remain), the world of man, with man as the chief actor, is incontestably the abiding subject of this sensationally mirrored flux. To exclude man and nature as organic surfaces, as the actual contexture of the social world, would be, for the movies, simply to give movement not to life as such, but to the canon which non-objective art has bestowed on life; to the non-mirroring wall-décor of extreme abstractionism . . . where man is not his own spectacle and where the only "recognizable" elements are atmosphere and geometric form.

Shall it be asked, now, whether it is necessary *for man to be his own spectacle?* Maybe human self-consciousness, for all its supposed glories, is actually a handicap; maybe it is not only unnecessary, maybe it is undesirable! Do not the moral disquisitions of the new existentialist schools of philosophy hint as much? Maybe human *existence* was a pretentious and arrogant error. Maybe, too, all that is the bad conscience of idealism itself—of man as consciously the perfectible being. I wish to suggest, nevertheless, that in failing to report man in the fluid grip of his historic fate as man, non-objectivism has created a gap in the texture of consciousness itself, which only the absolute withdrawal of the individual from the world can adequately mend. This is doubtless a prejudiced, though not necessarily an inflexible, view of the values of non-objective painting. Possibly there should be, as there are and have been, moments of *human* as well as *individual* self-negation. But is not such self-negation always the function of thought itself?—and does not the crude experience of the world supply it aside from all reaching toward aesthetic feelings and artistic creation? Maybe the "gap" is inherent in consciousness. But objectively, blank walls and the void have always supplied this gap, and oftener than one may like; philosophy is its traditional antidote, art its traditional mirror. Maybe non-objective paintings are so many portraits of the void in its fluid and static moods. . . . But such a "portrait art"—a mirror of its own—would seem, in comparison with the whole of human experience, both narrow and tending to barrenness. I suggest that the lowly movies are, after all, a positive antidote to this extreme convention of modern painting; that even the banes of commercial films, the super-spectacle and the mad melodrama, are athletic fields where the classic human image continues to prove its eligibility in the Olympiad of the art forms.

141